AF572479

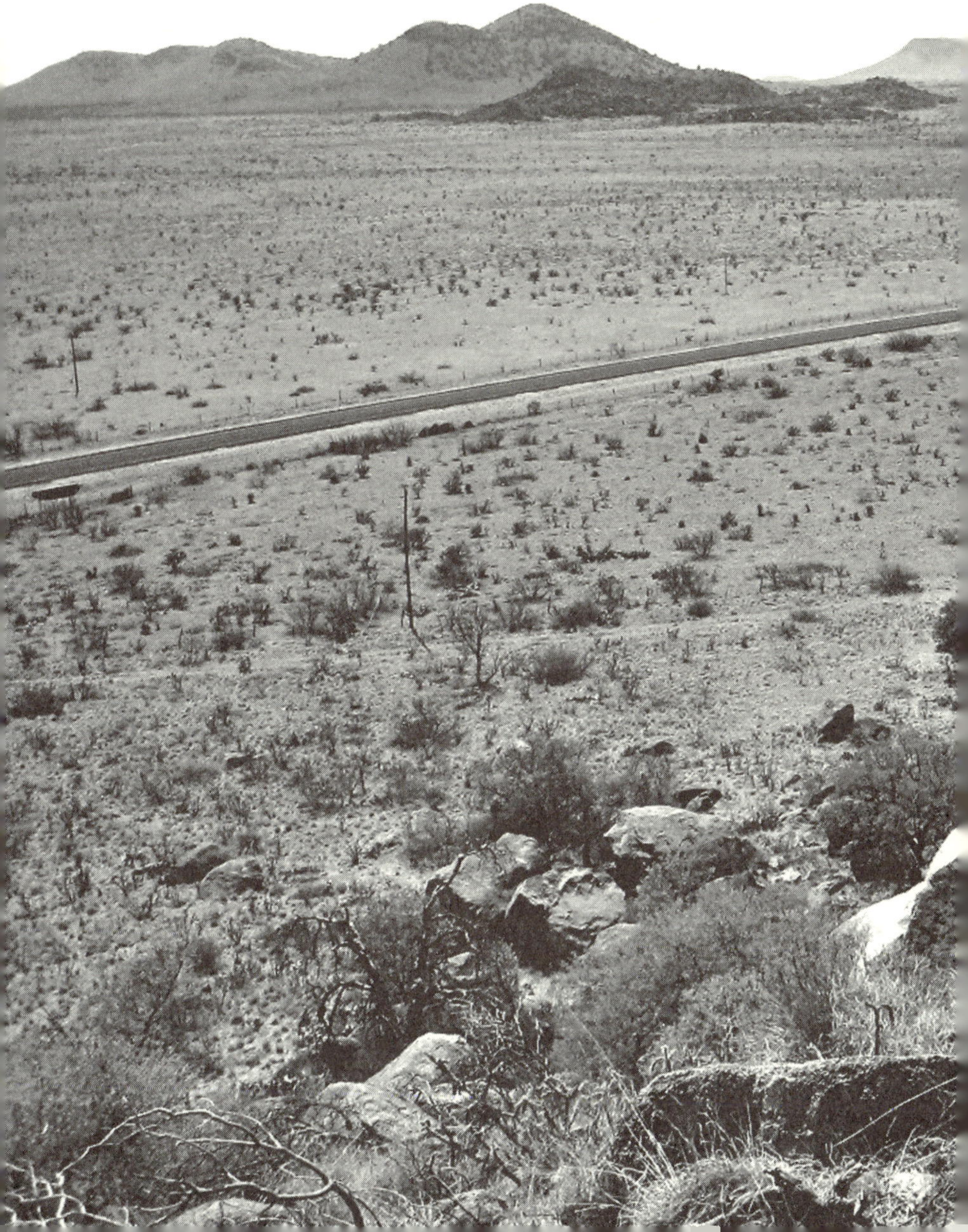

JOSHUA EDWARDS

EDITION SOLITUDE
REIHE PROJEKTIV

PHOTOGRAPHS TAKEN AT ONE-HOUR INTERVALS
DURING A WALK FROM GALVESTON ISLAND
TO THE WEST TEXAS TOWN OF MARFA

Photographs Taken at One-Hour Intervals During a Walk from Galveston Island to the West Texas Town of Marfa

PUBLISHER: Akademie Schloss Solitude, Jean-Baptiste Joly
AUTHOR/PHOTOGRAPHER: Joshua Edwards
DESIGN: Gou Dao Niao
PAPER: 60# Natural Recycled
FONTS: Apex New and Charter BT Pro
COVER: "West Texas Landscape, March 26, 2012"
Edition of 1000 copies
ISBN 978-3-937158-76-1

Printed in the United States of America
by McNaughton & Gunn, Inc.

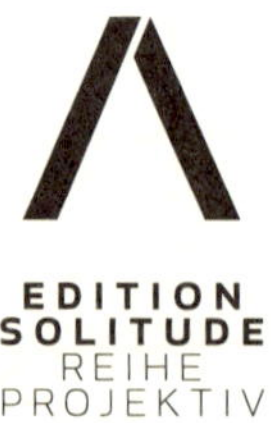

EDITION
SOLITUDE
REIHE
PROJEKTIV

Akademie Schloss Solitude
Solitude 3. 70197 Stuttgart
Germany

for my parents

INTRODUCTION

On November 10th, having just returned to the States from a year in Germany, with time on my hands and without a job or anywhere to call home, I set out on foot from my birthplace on Galveston Island, heading to the West Texas town of Marfa, where Lynn Xu and I will build a house and settle down after many years of moving around. I followed the coast for two days, then turned inland at Surfside, passing through West Columbia, Needville, East Bernard, Eagle Lake, Columbus, La Grange, Buescher State Park, and Bastrop before arriving in Austin, where Lynn was waiting to join me. Together we walked through Dripping Springs, Johnson City, Stonewall, and Fredericksburg on our way to Kerrville, where we spent Thanksgiving with my family. Lynn had to leave on a trip to California, and I headed out again after five days of rest, accompanied by a friend to Junction, then onward alone through Sonora, Ozona, Iraan, and Fort Stockton. From there I turned southwest, and my father met up with me on the road to walk a dozen miles into Alpine. The next day, December 20th, three friends accompanied me for the final leg, and I arrived in Marfa two hours past sunset, forty days after beginning. Throughout the journey I took one photograph each hour. The first image is of the building that now stands in the place of the hospital where I was born, and the last, taken in the morning light on the day after I reached town, is of the property where Lynn and I will live: 404 West Galveston Street in Marfa. This book collects the trip's 230 photographs and serves as a companion to a volume of poems and prose, *Architecture for Travelers*, and to an overarching experiment of the same name, which will be finished when our house is built. These books, as well as the ongoing project, are made possible by the sponsorship of the Akademie Schloss Solitude and by supportive friends and family, whose ideas and kindness have provided the energy and purpose to go forth.

— Joshua Edwards

MAP

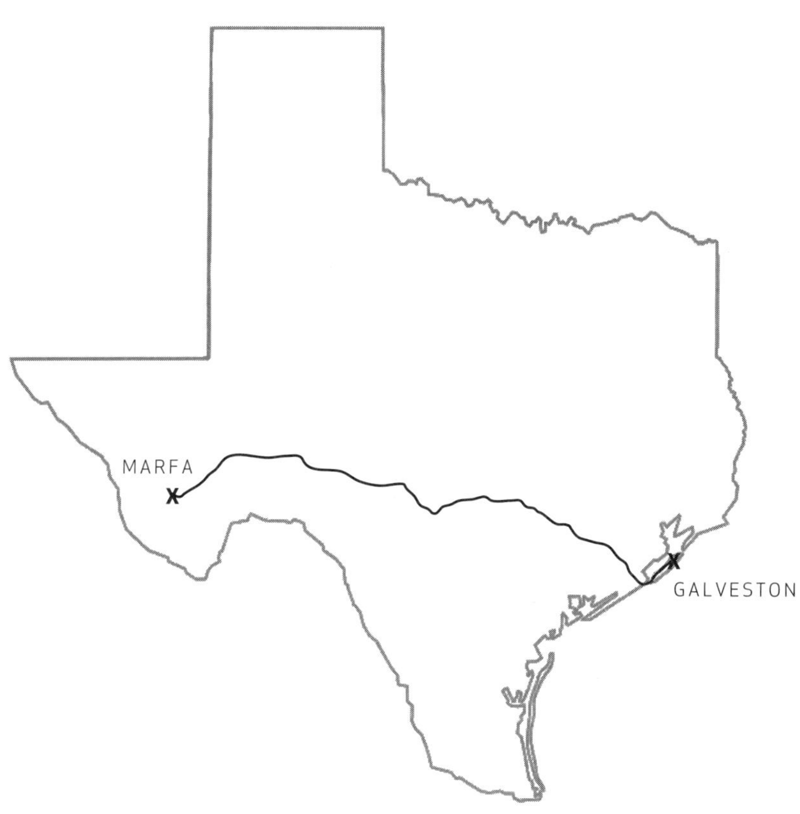

The earth was all symbol.

—Lynn Xu, "Earth Light"

PHOTOGRAPHS TAKEN AT ONE-HOUR INTERVALS DURING A WALK FROM GALVESTON ISLAND TO THE WEST TEXAS TOWN OF MARFA

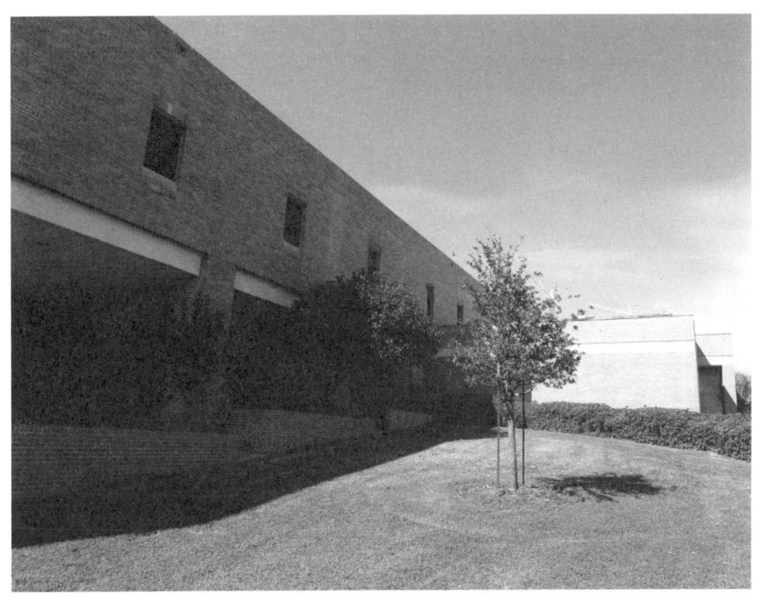

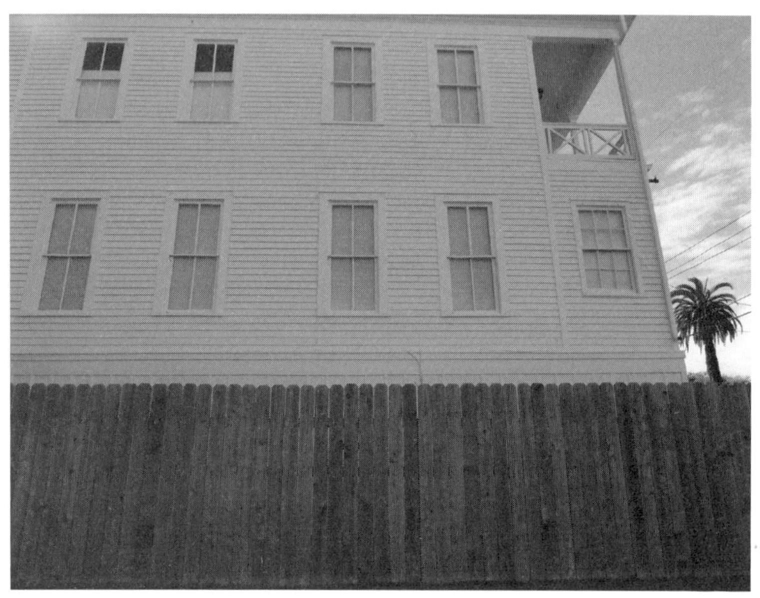

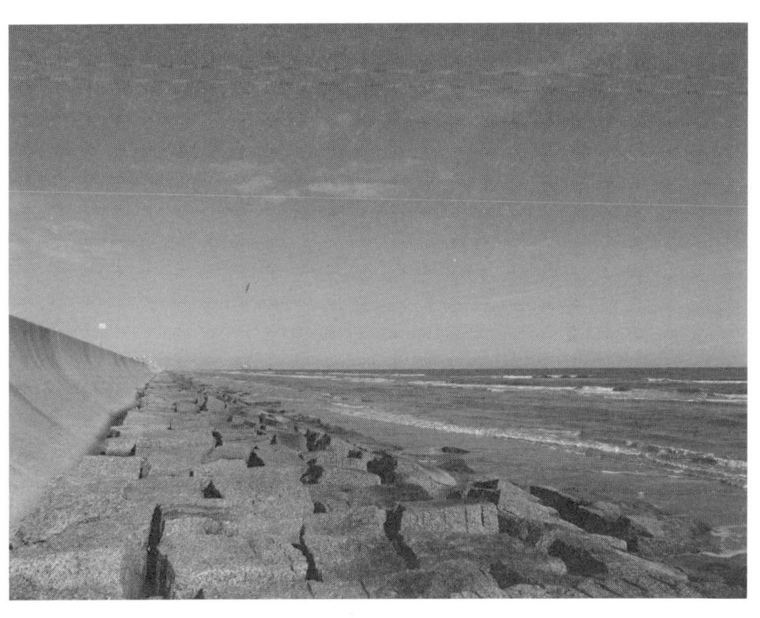

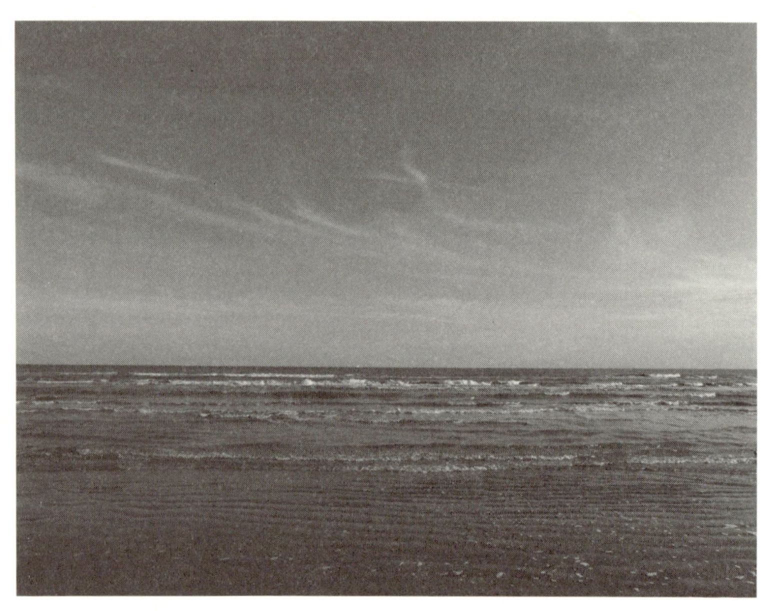

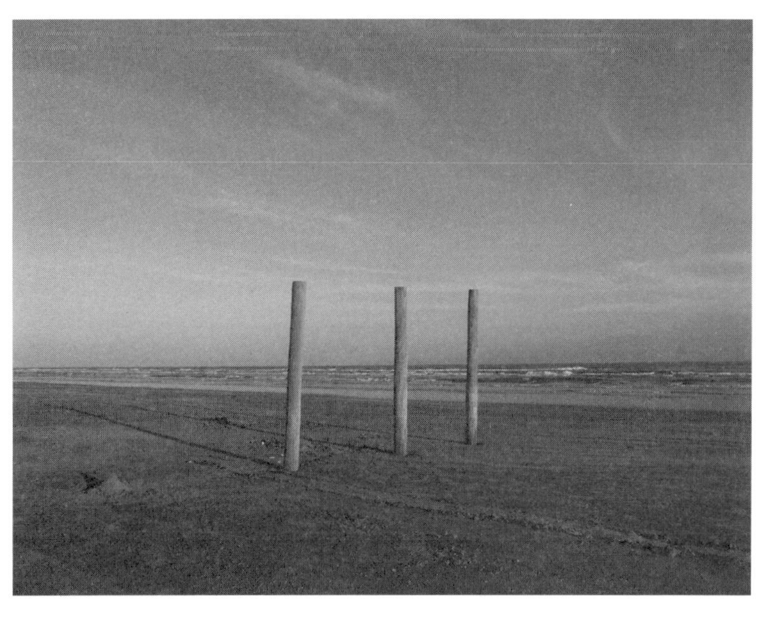

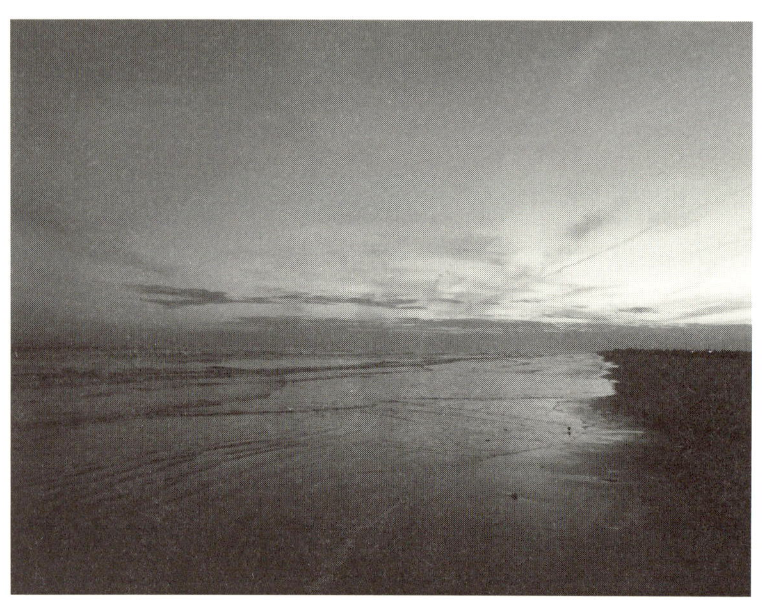

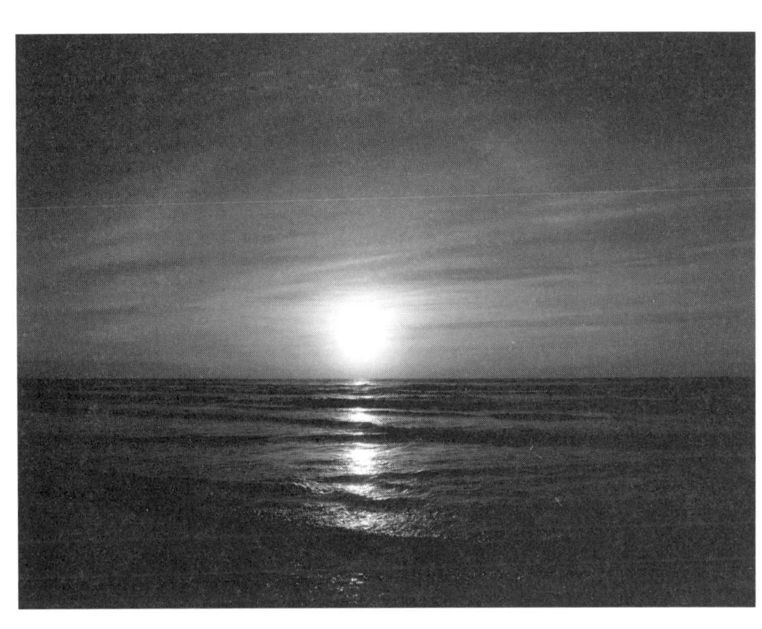

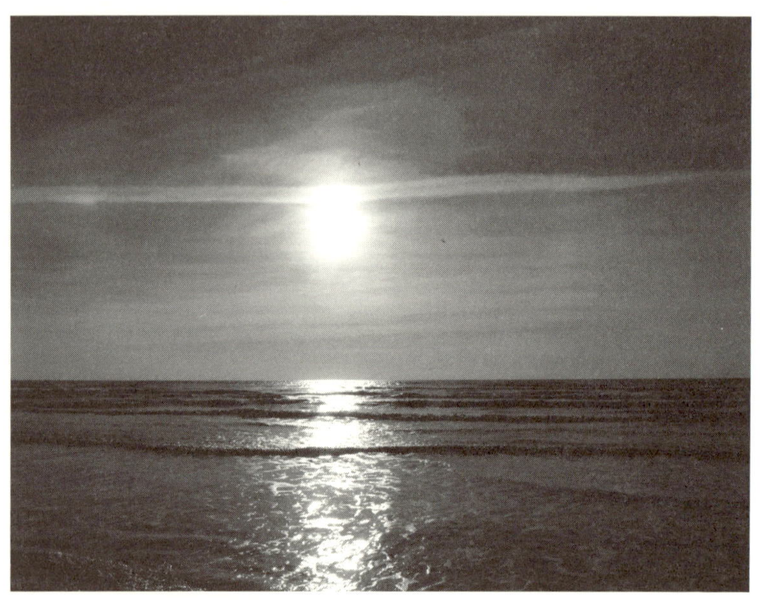

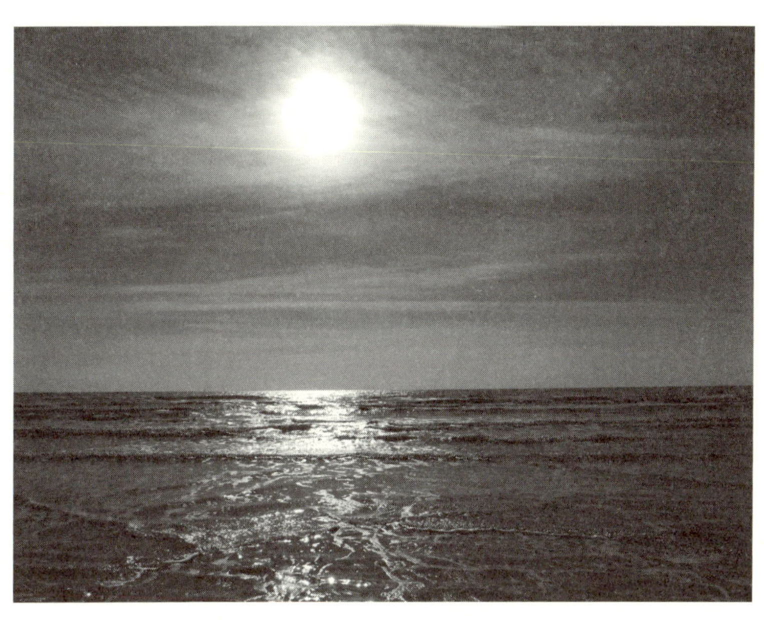

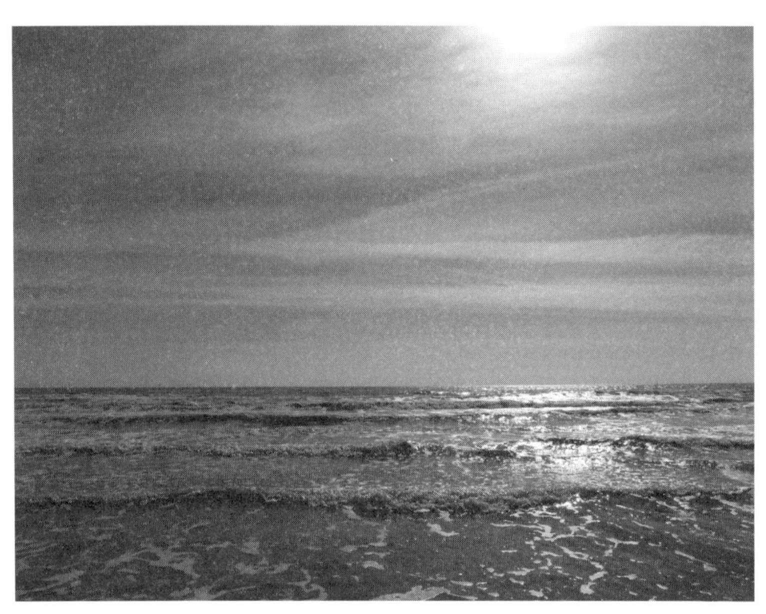

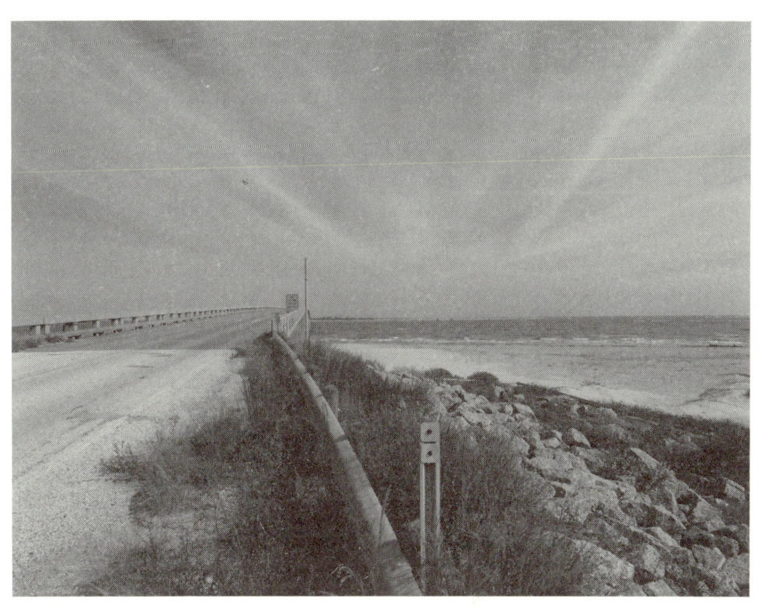

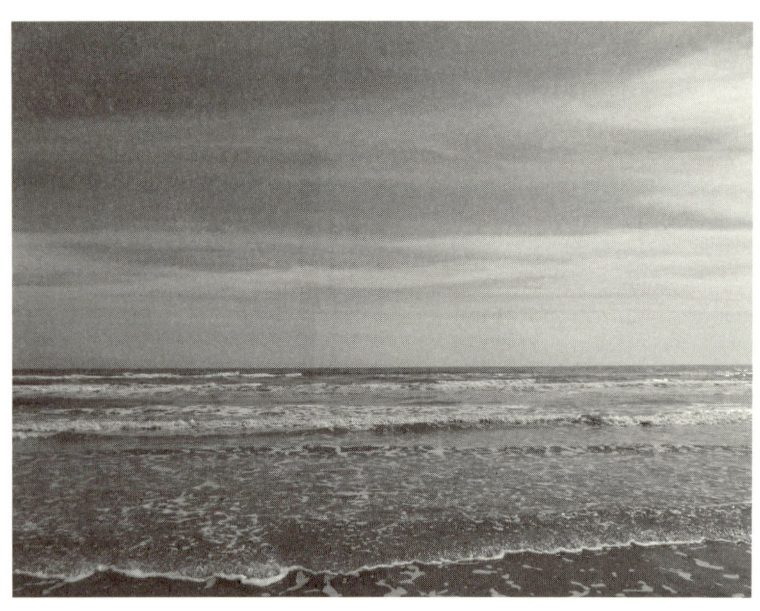

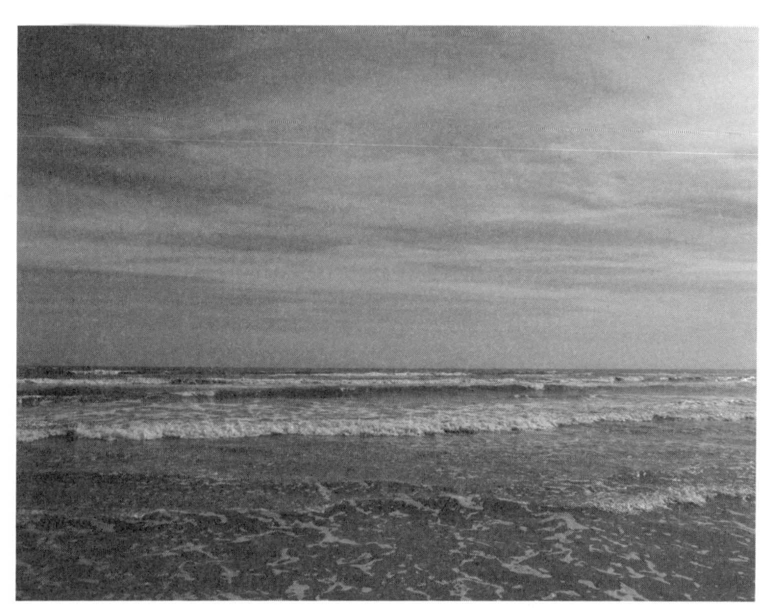

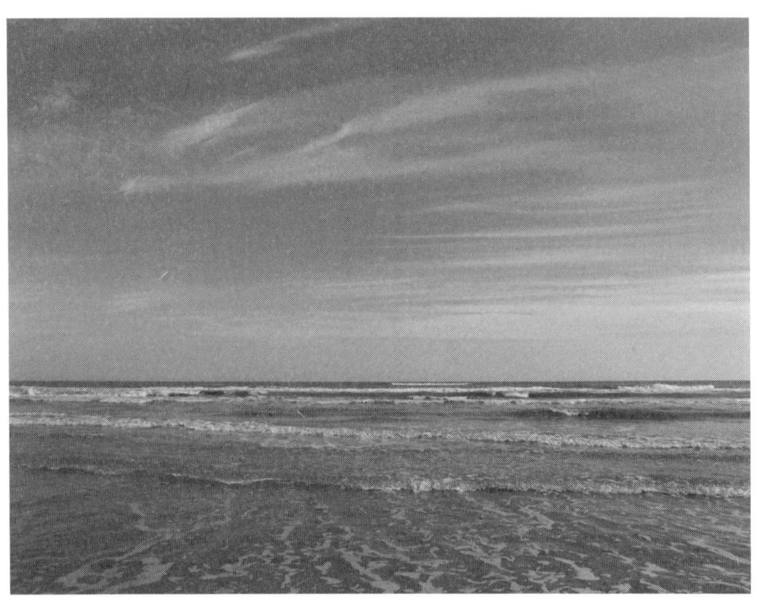

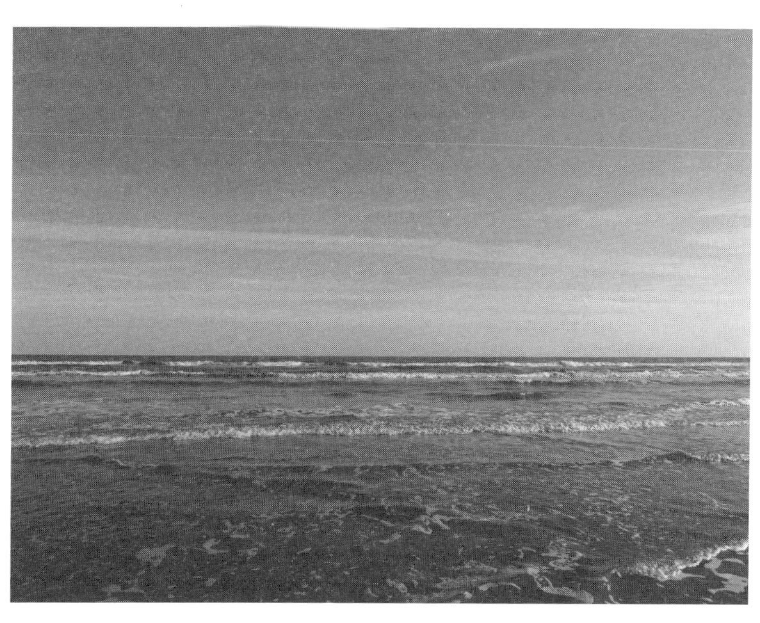

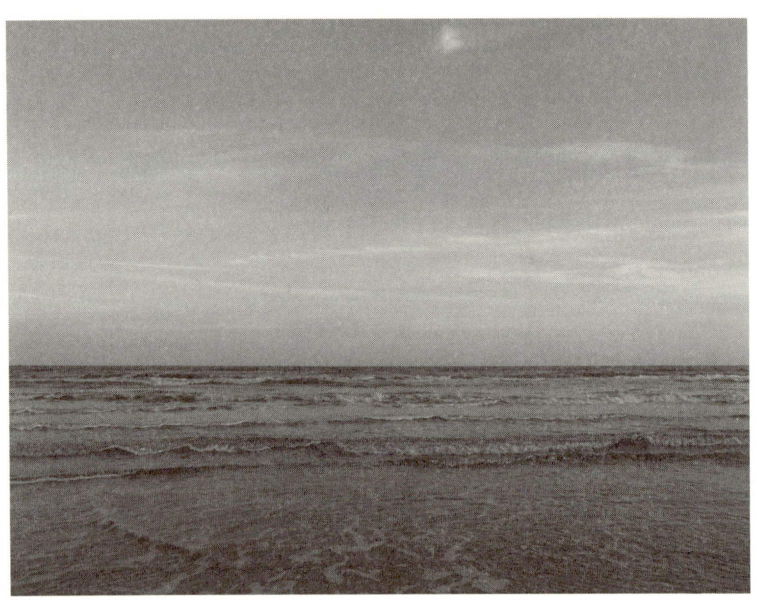

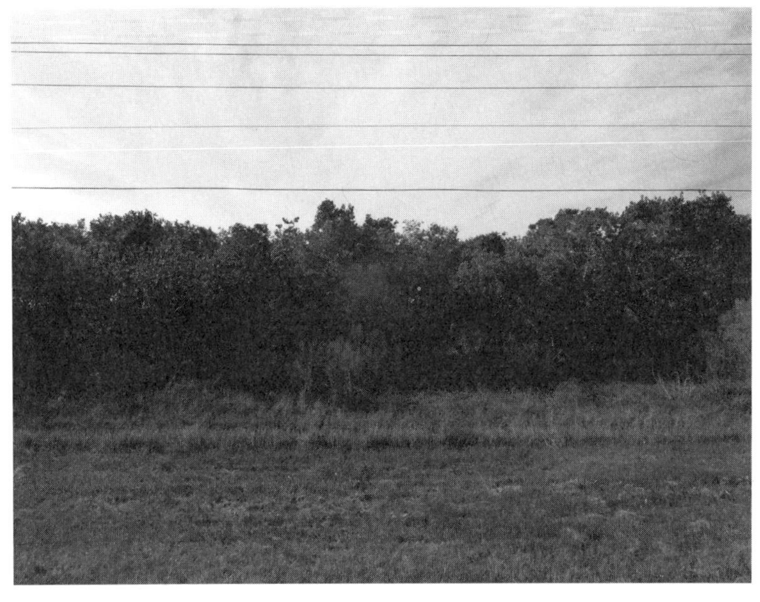

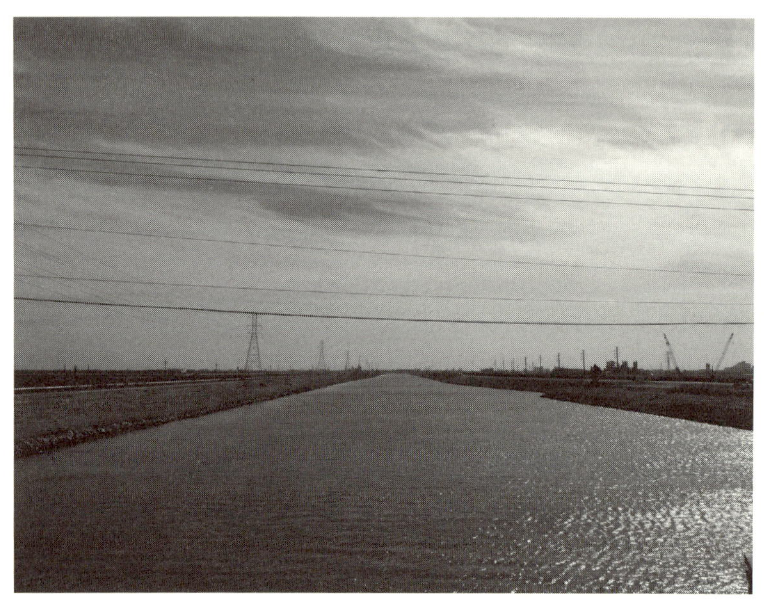

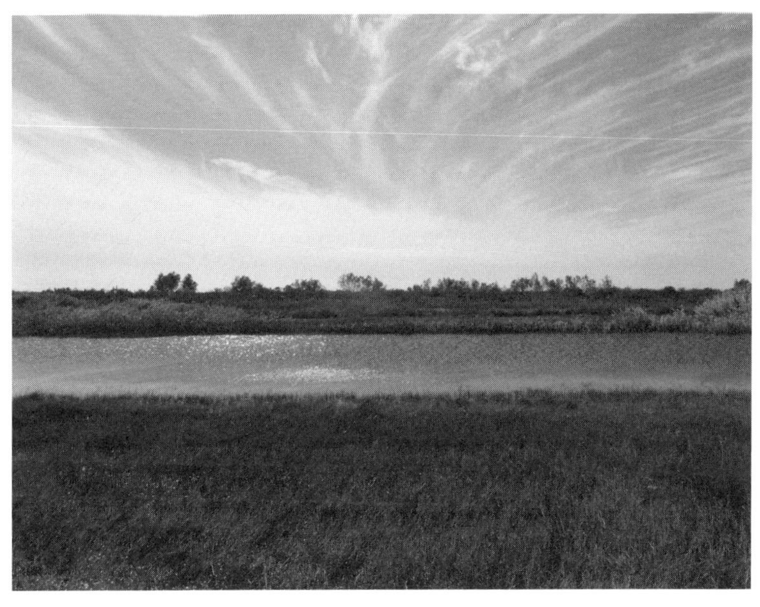

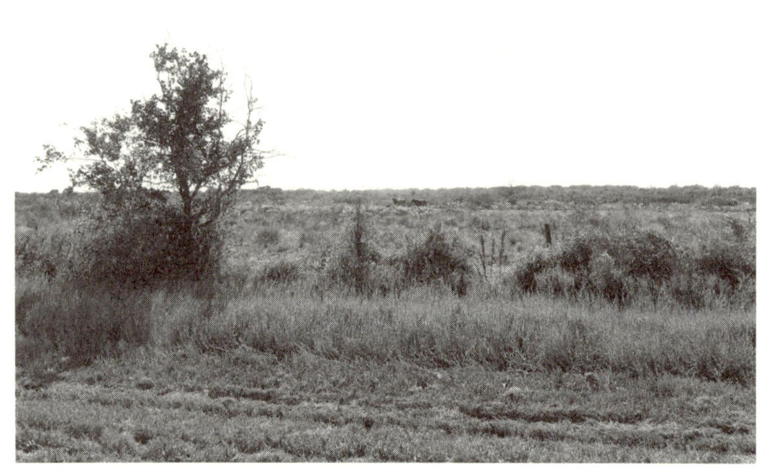

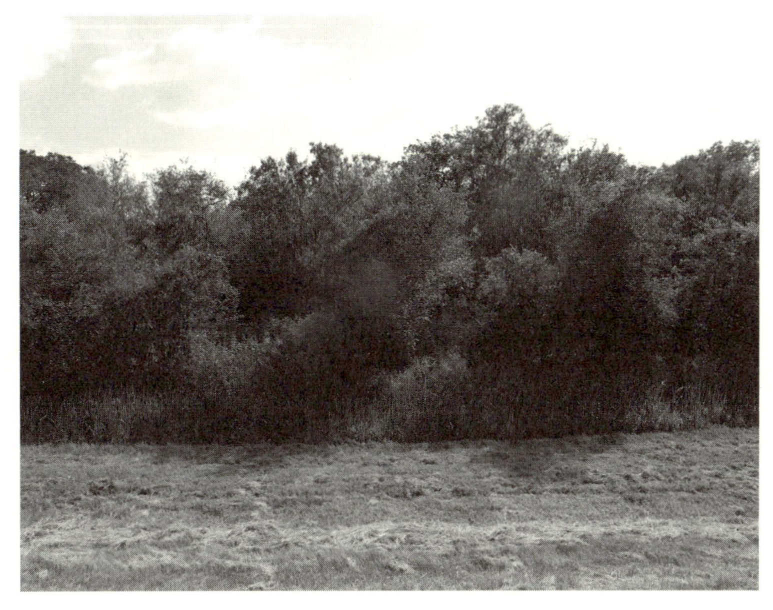

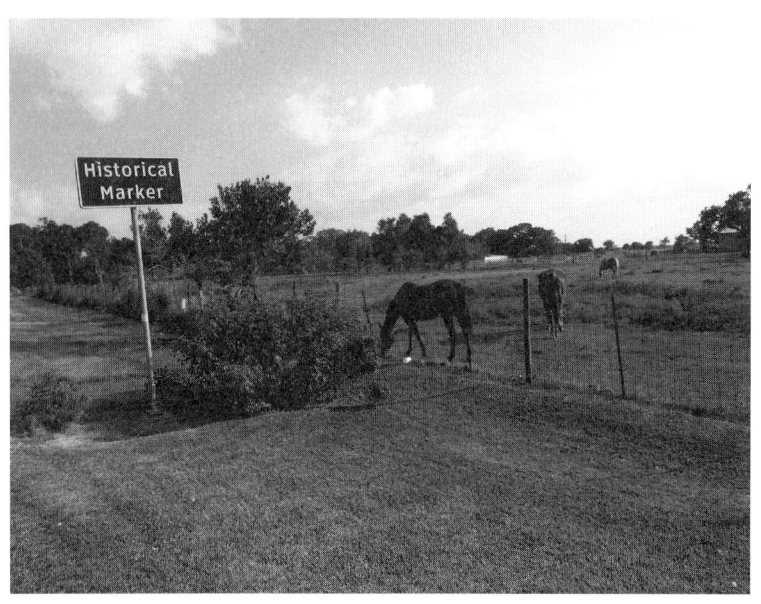
Historical
Marker

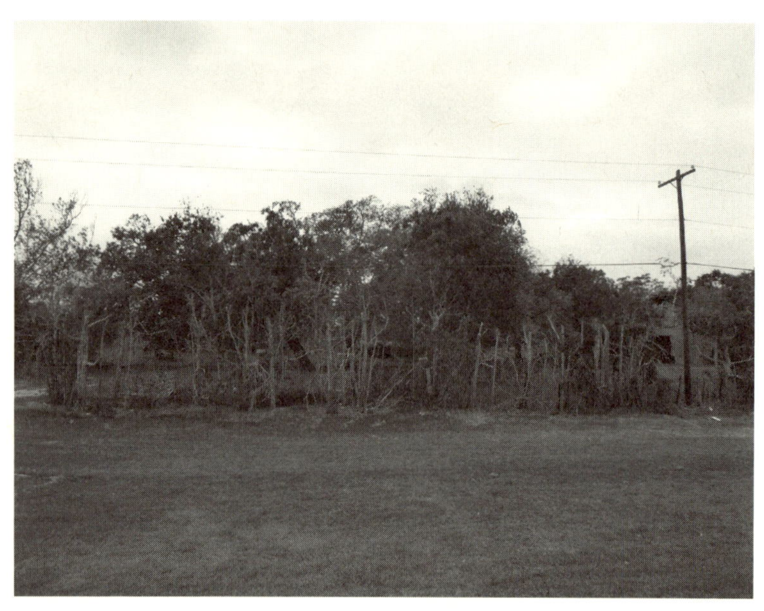

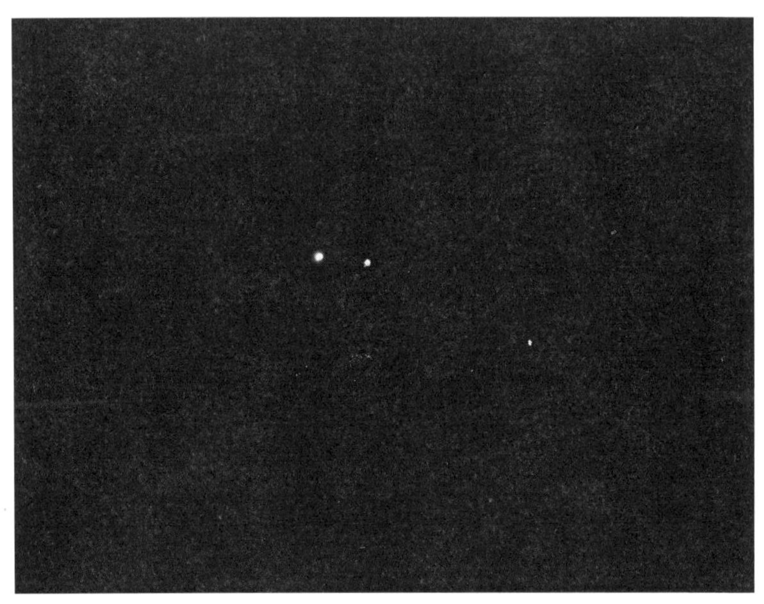

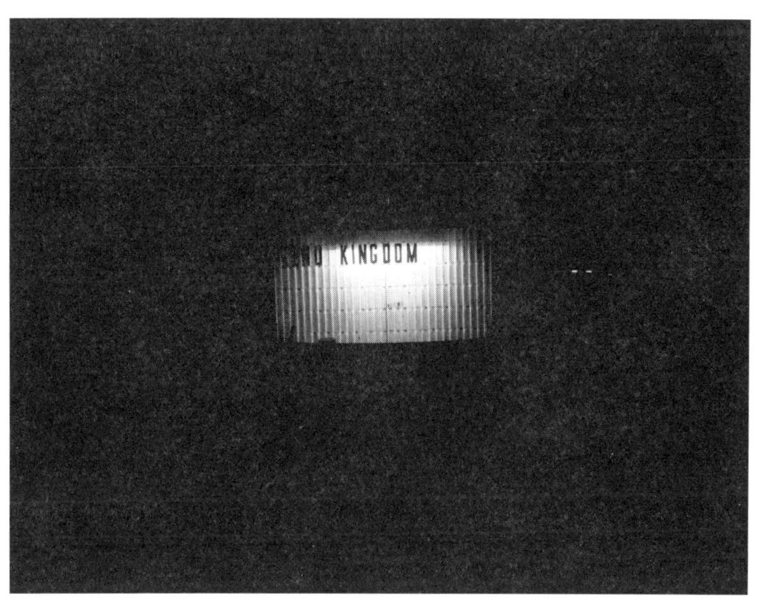
KINGDOM

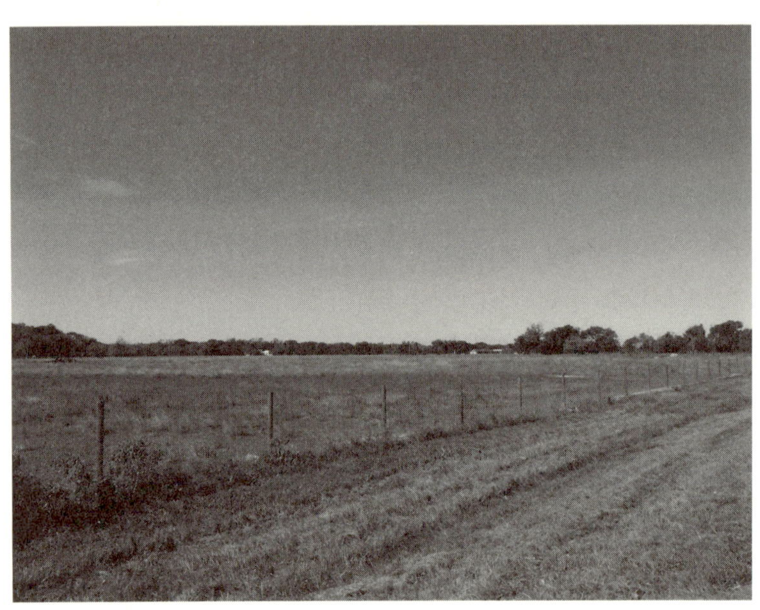

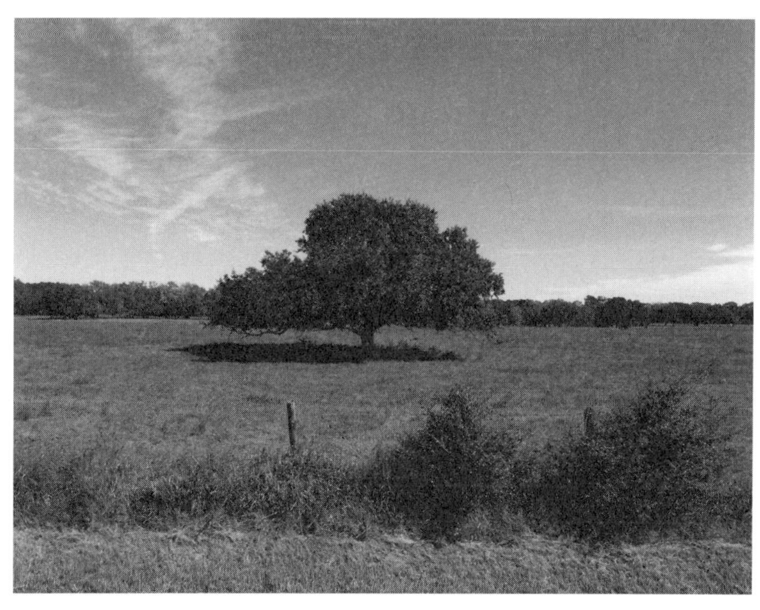

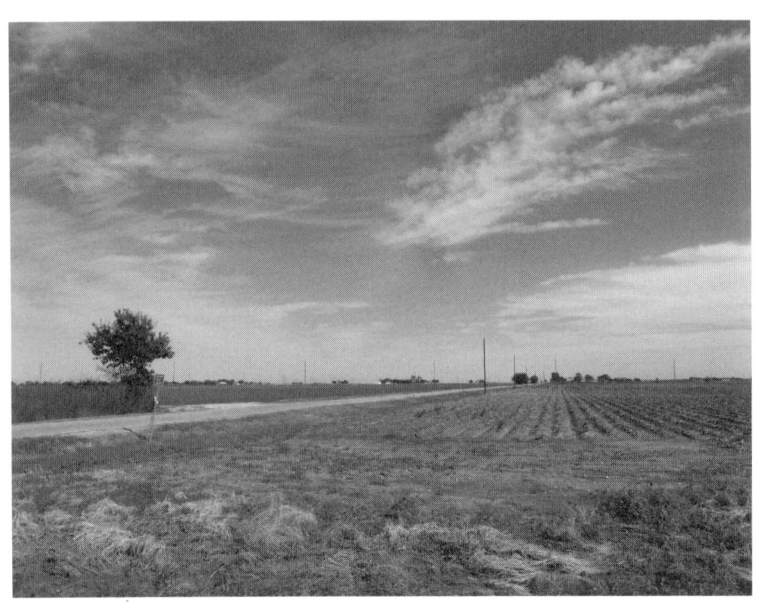

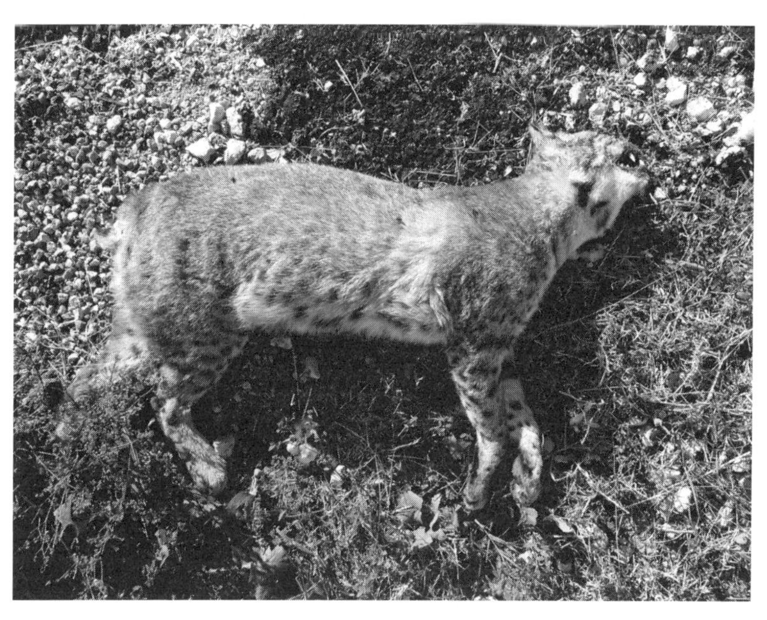

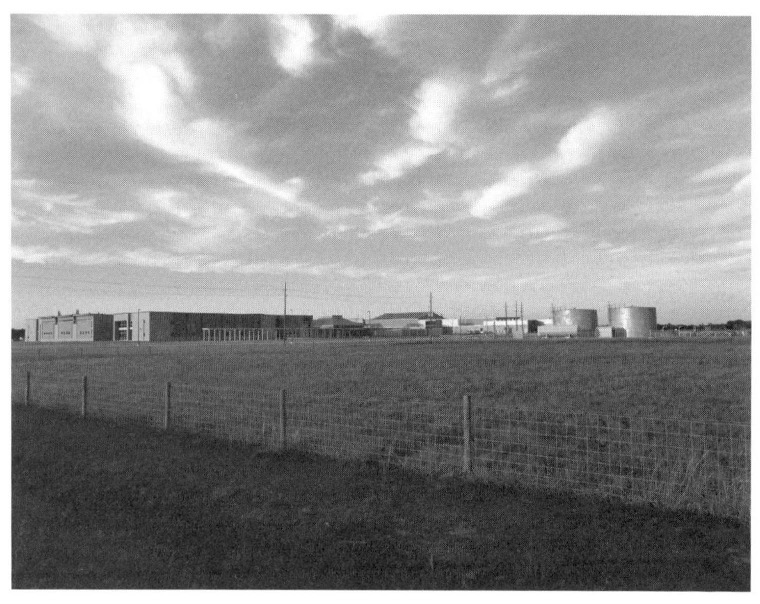

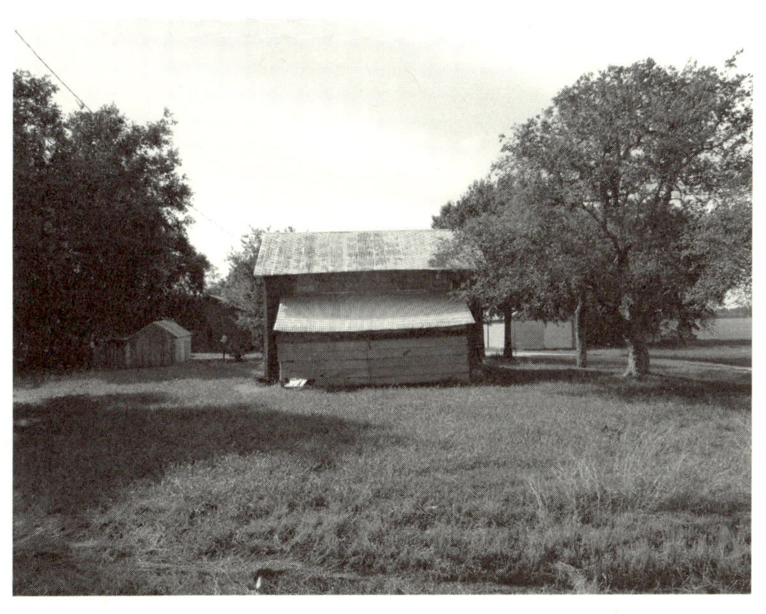

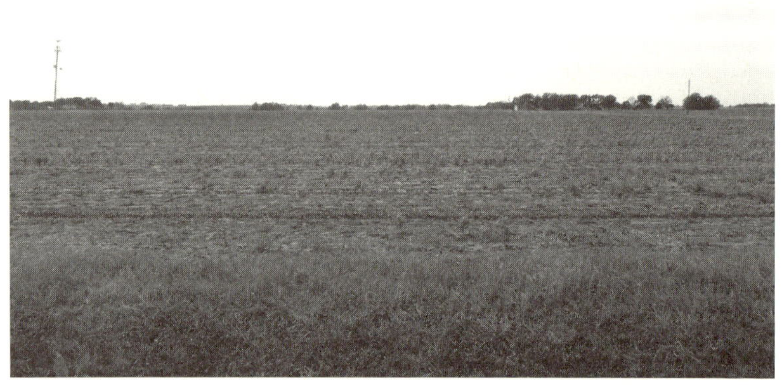

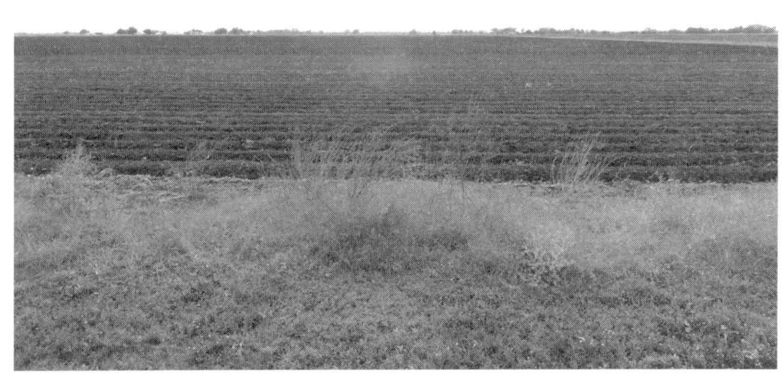

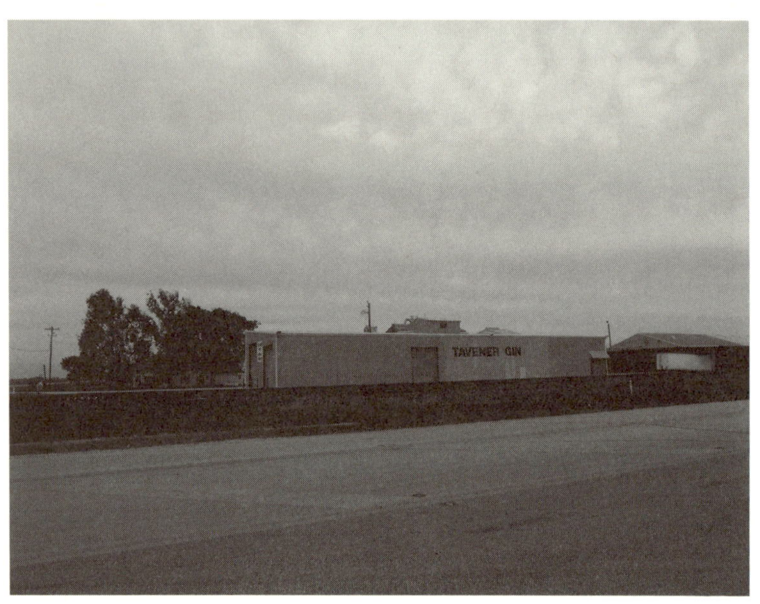
TAVENER GIN

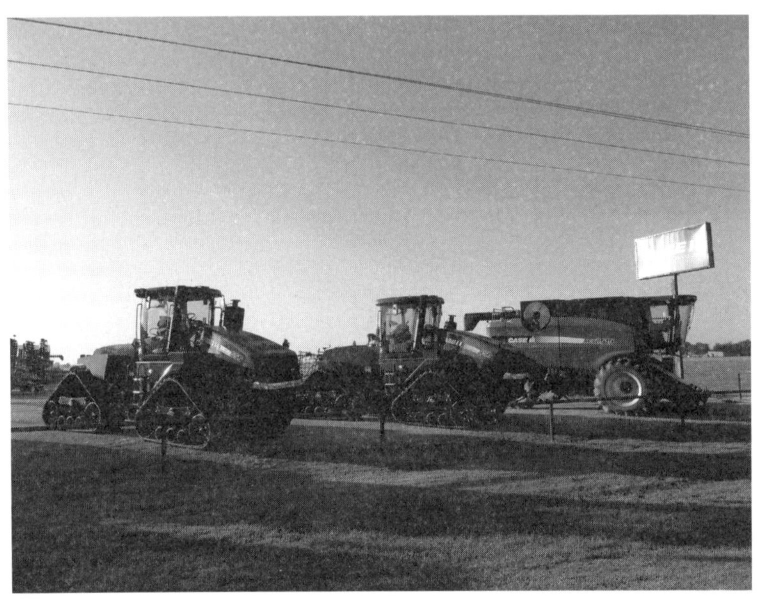
CASE IH

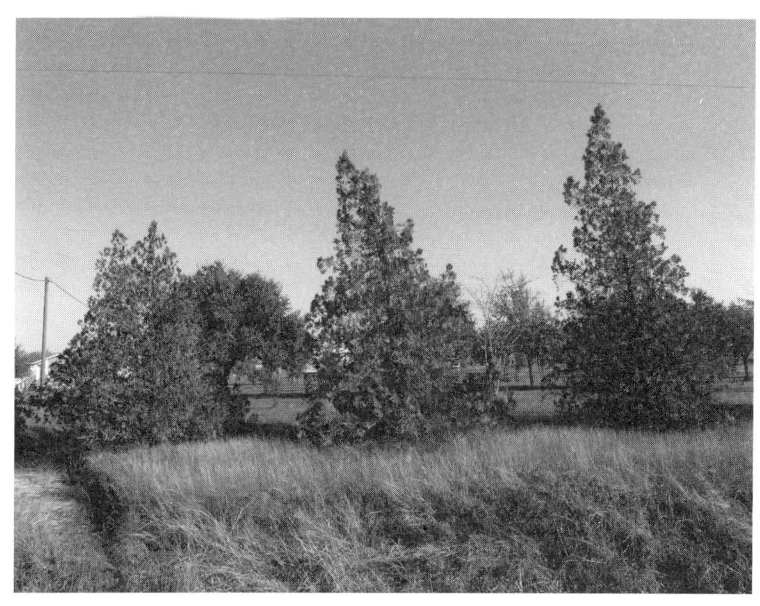

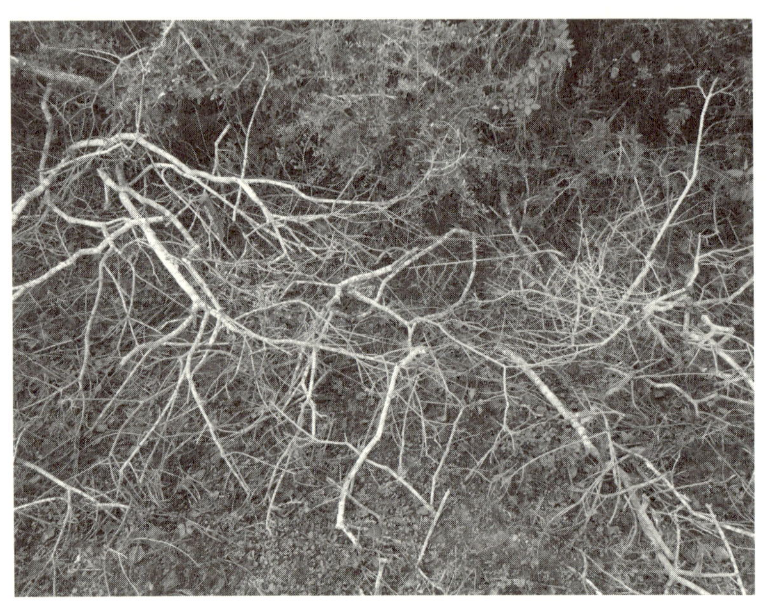

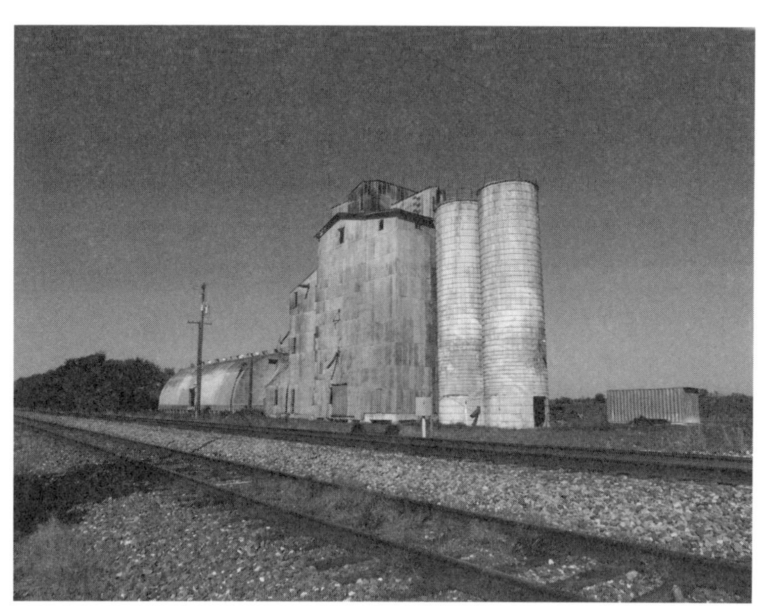

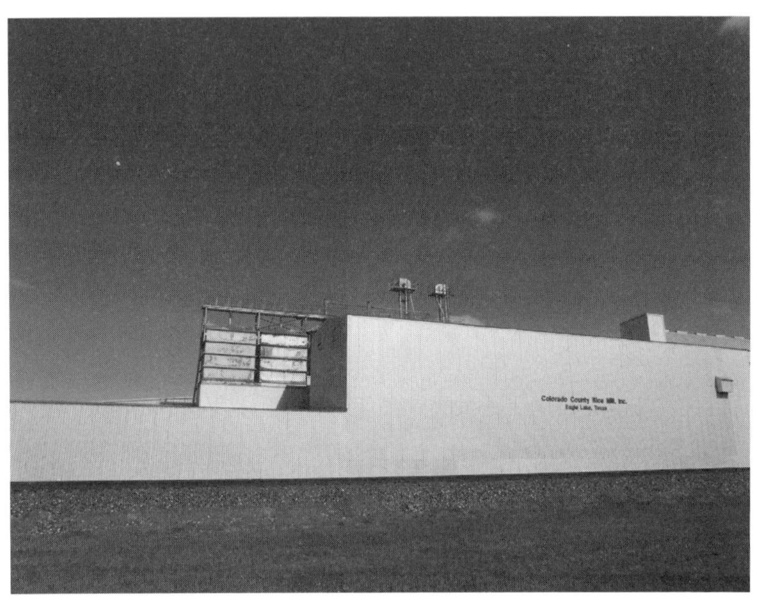

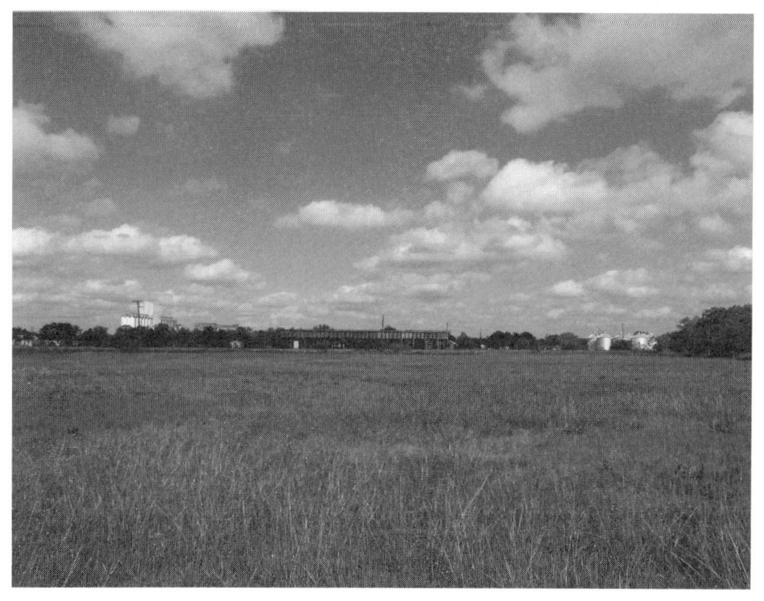

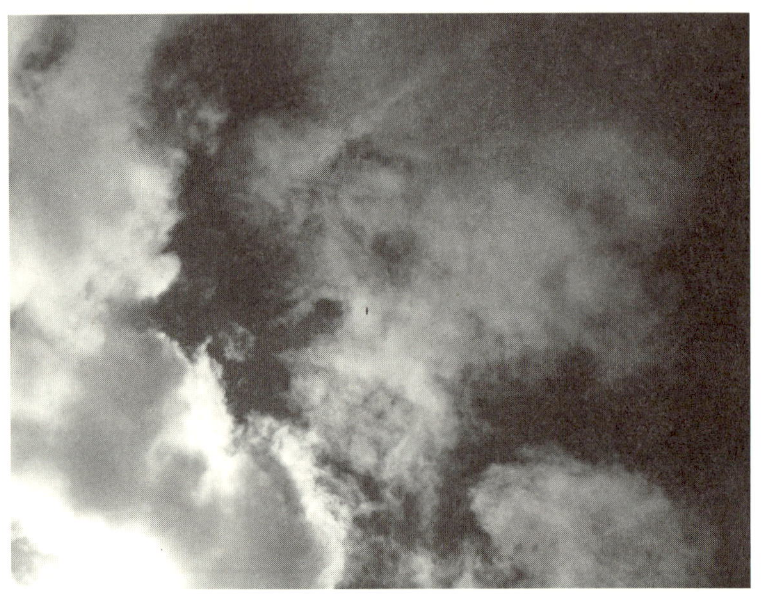

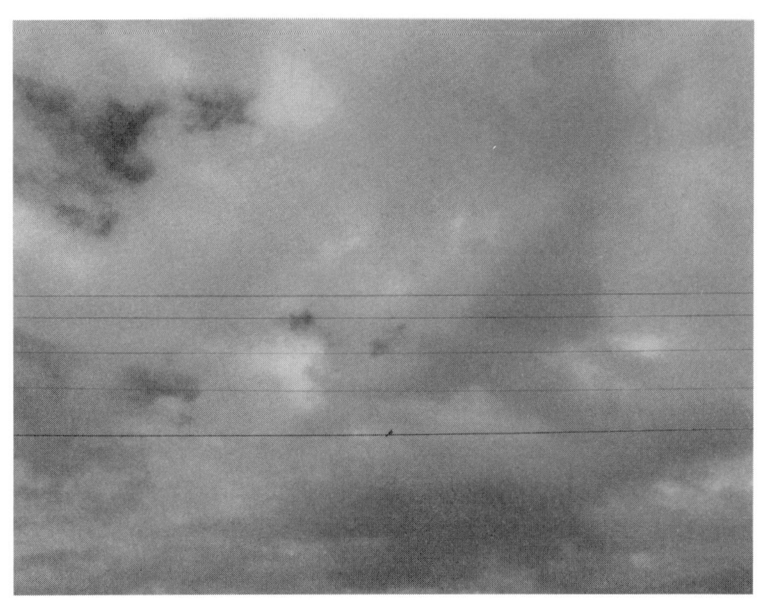

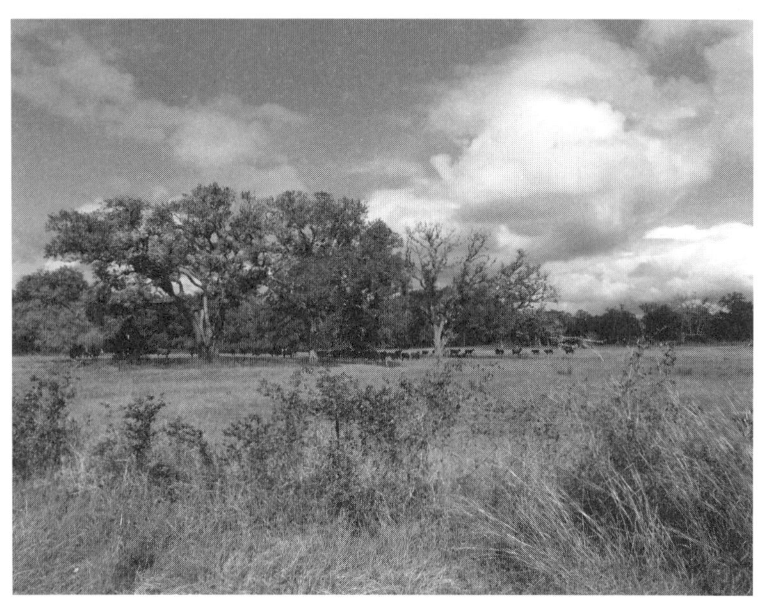

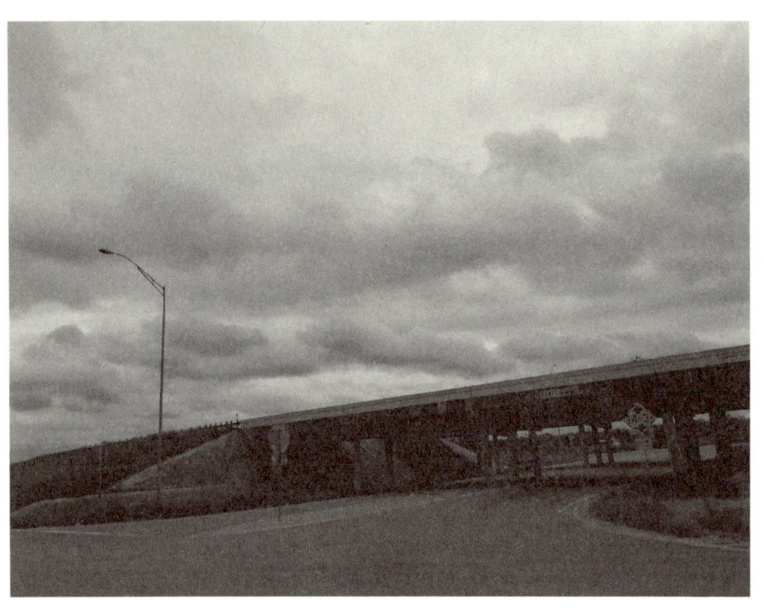

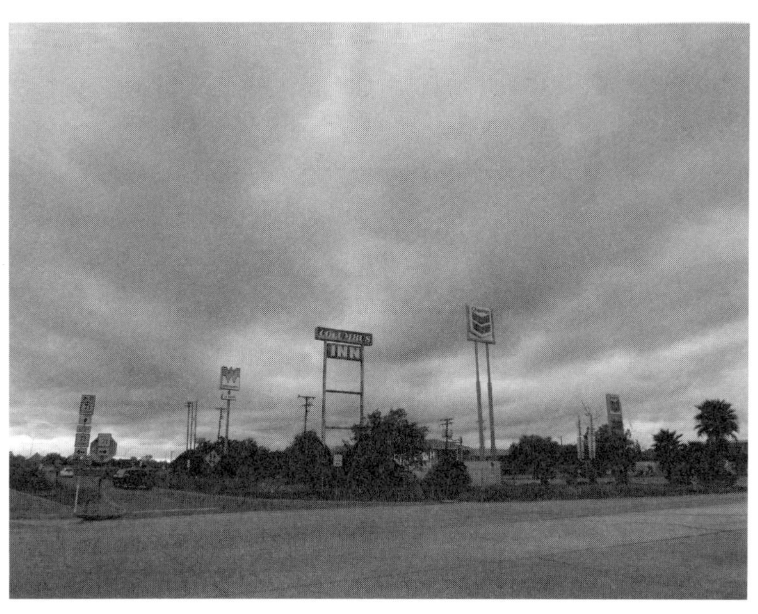
INN

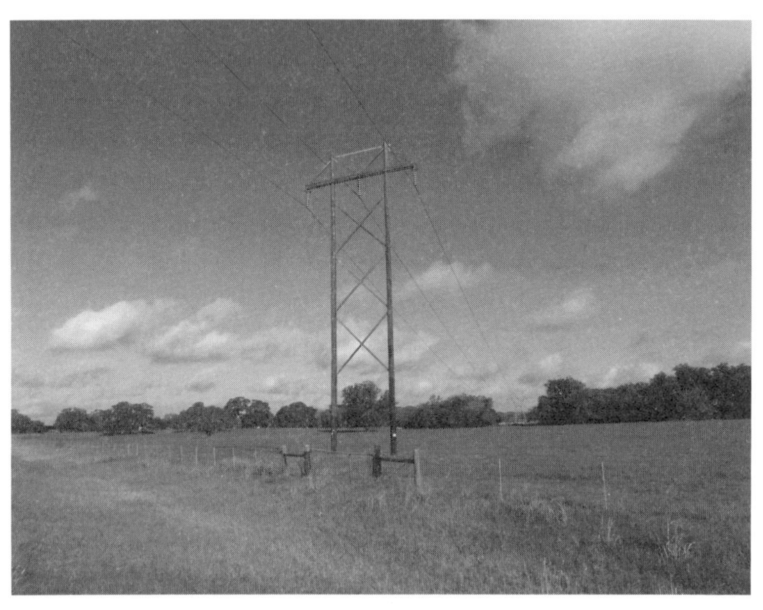

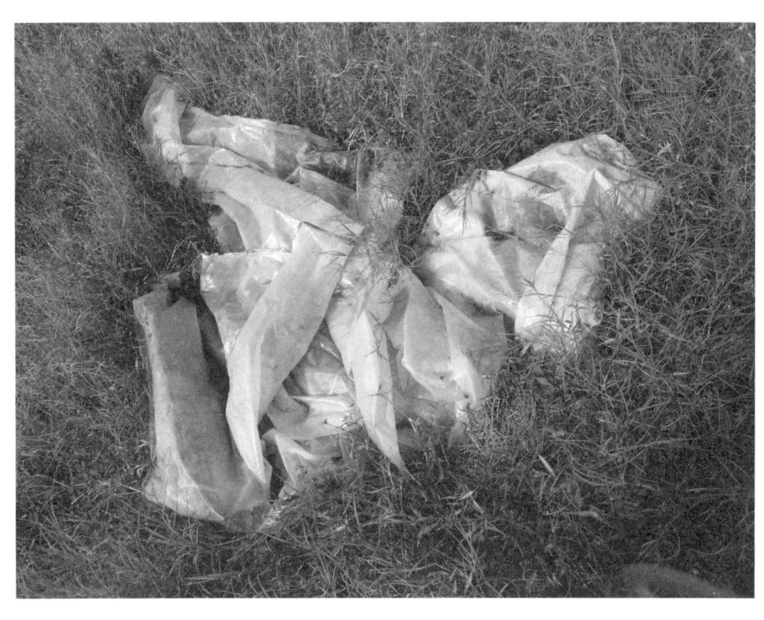

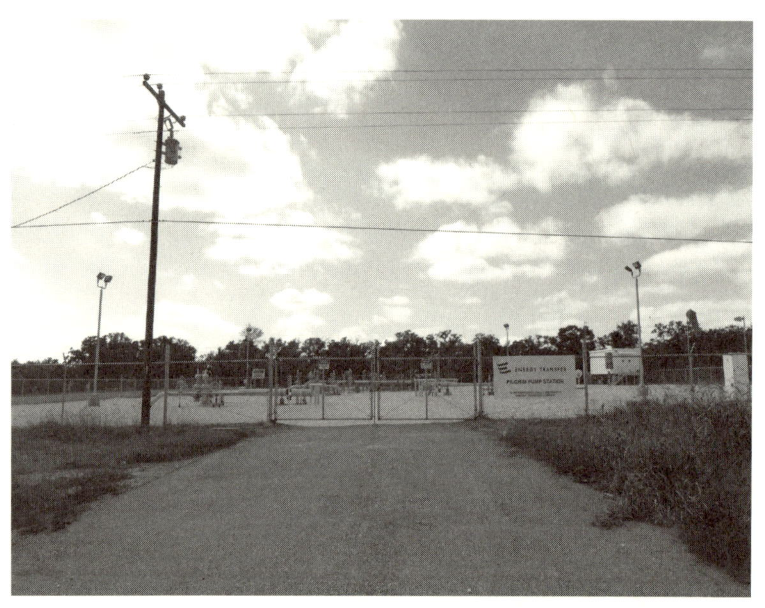
ENERGY TRANSFER
PILGRIM PUMP STATION

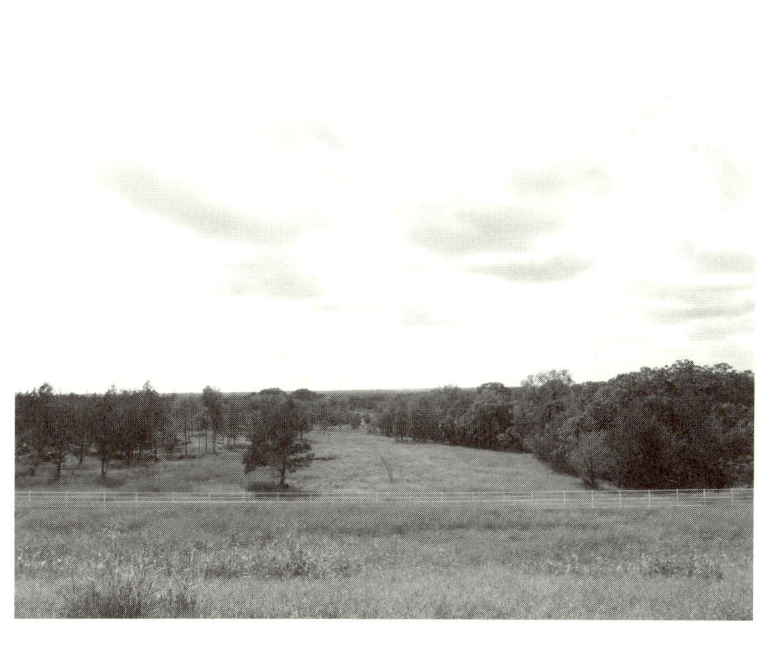

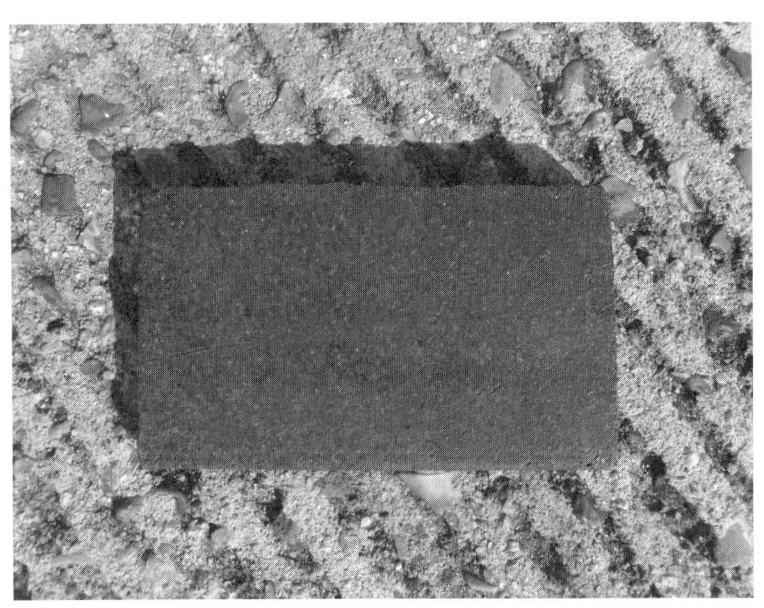

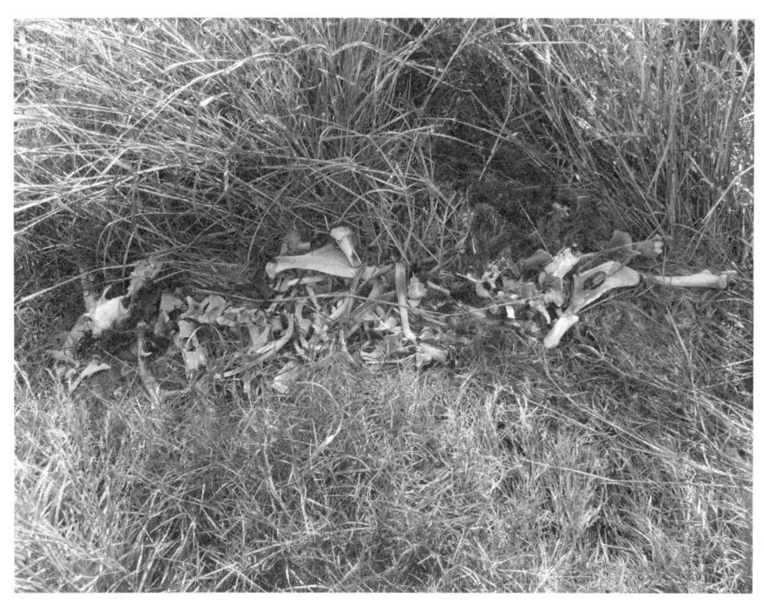

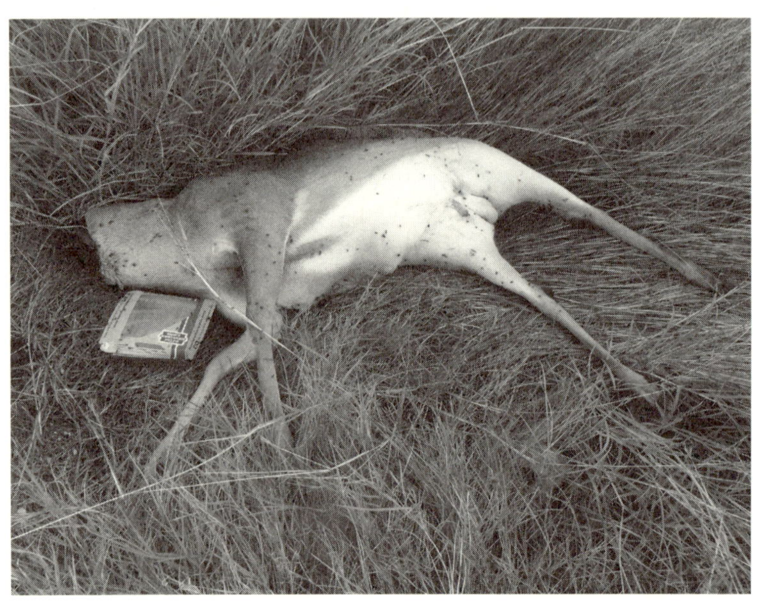

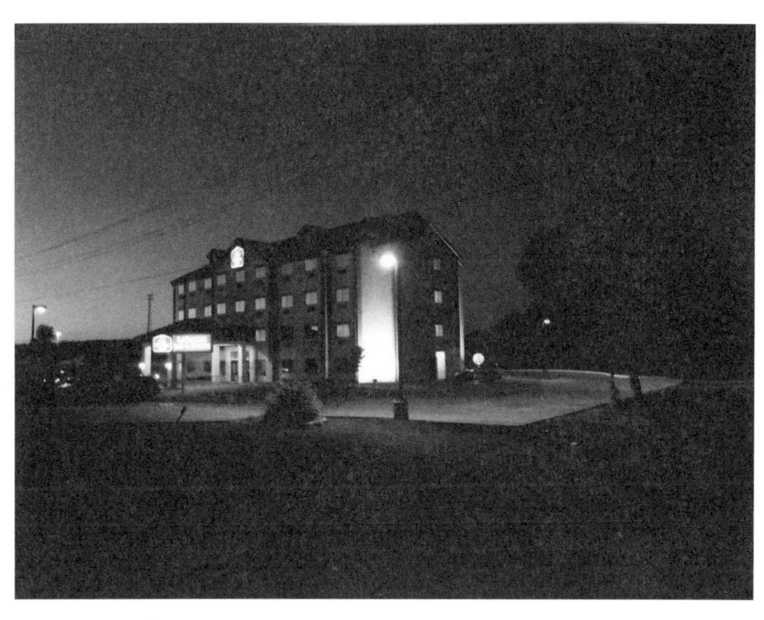

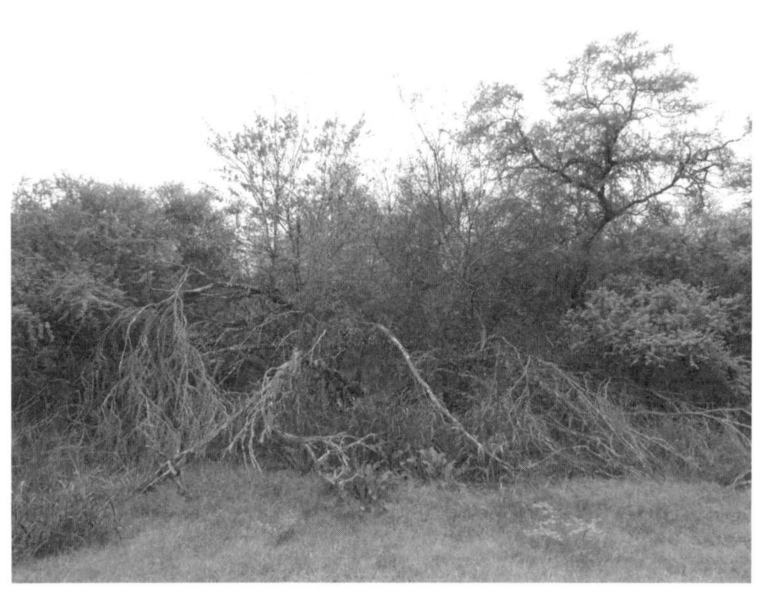

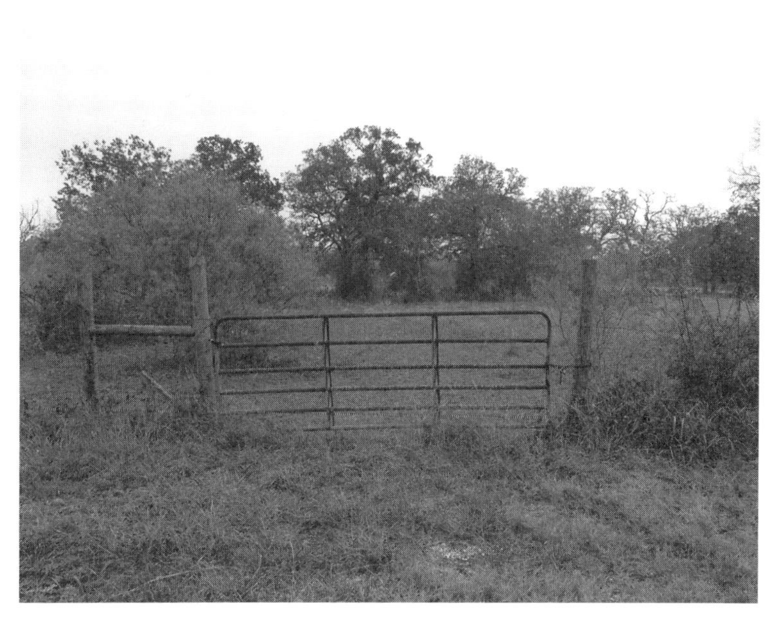

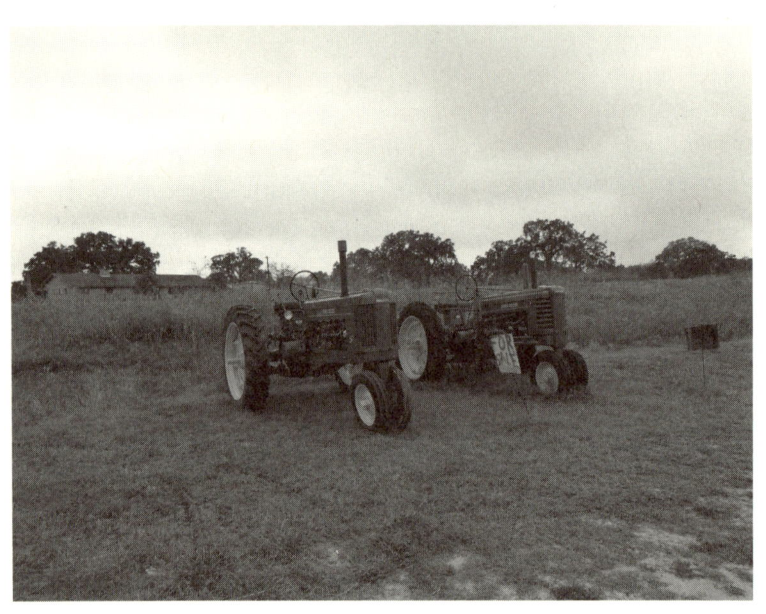

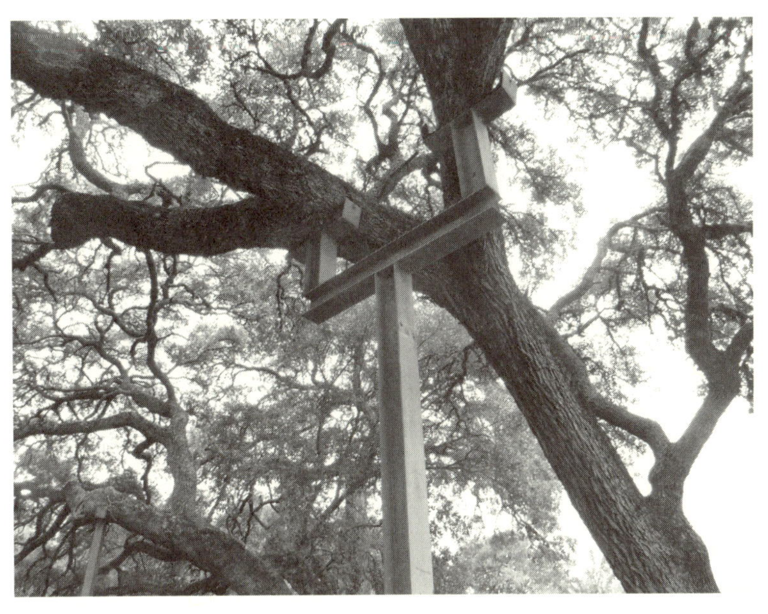

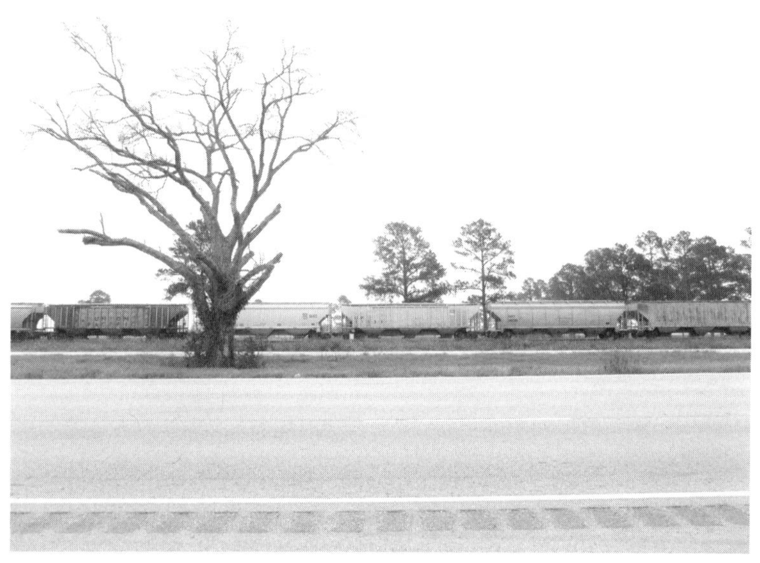

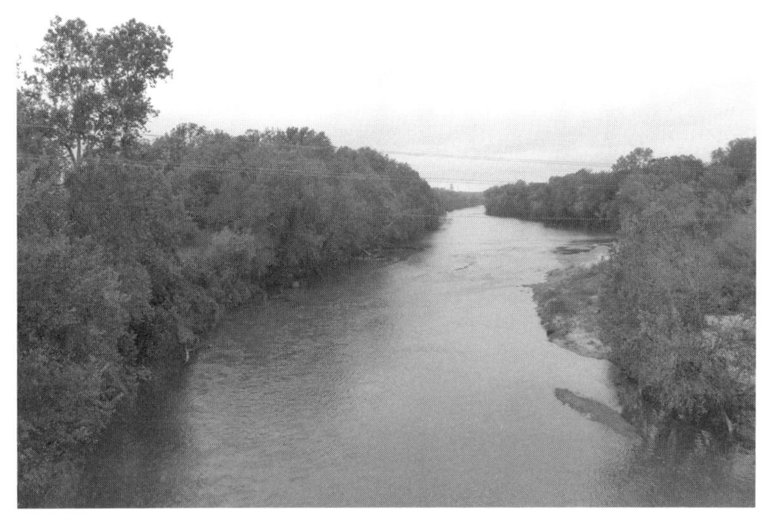

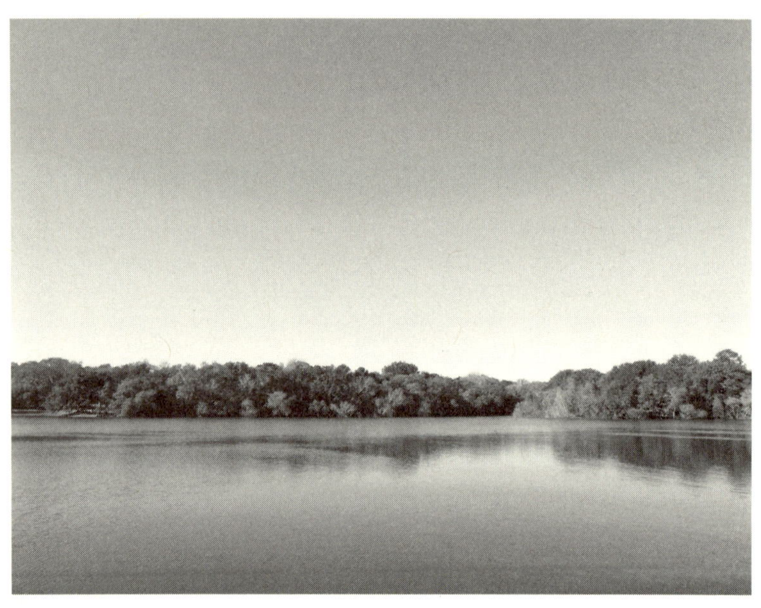

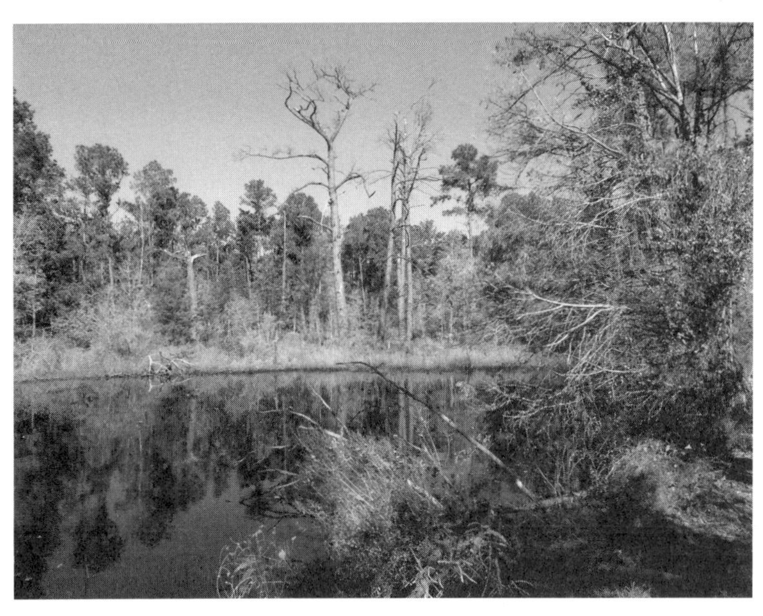

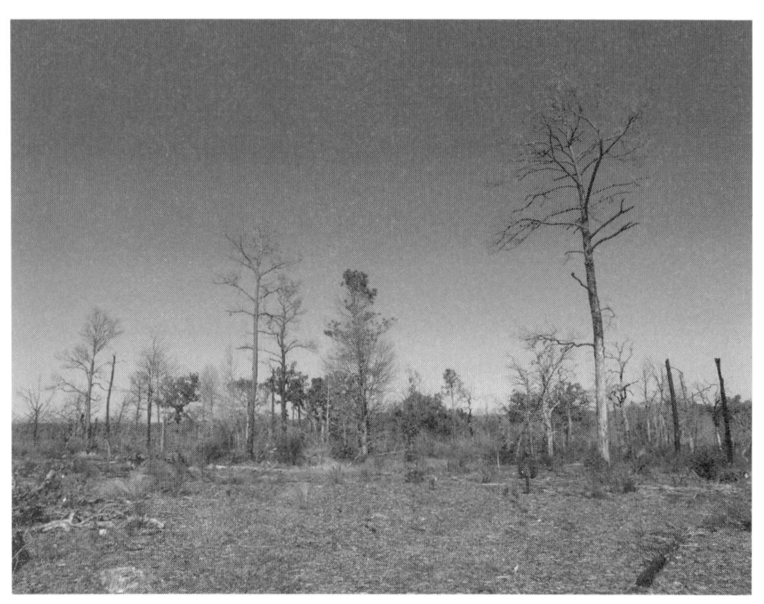

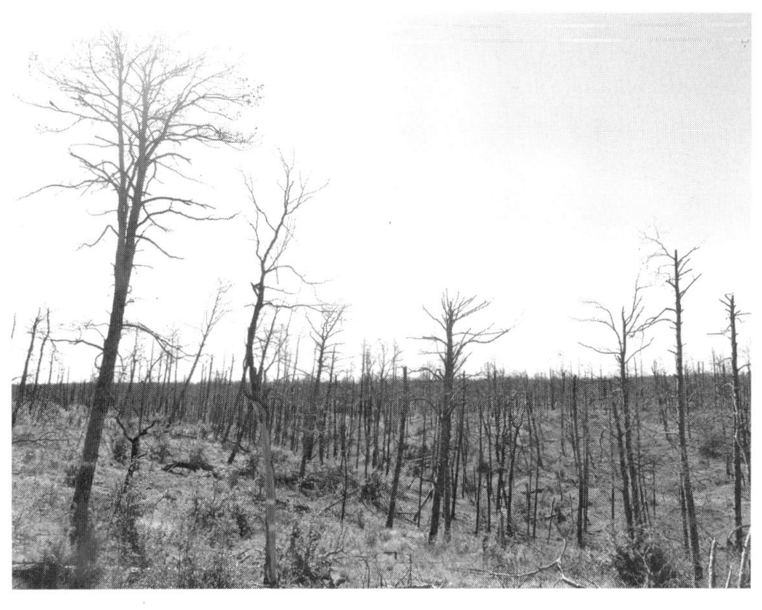

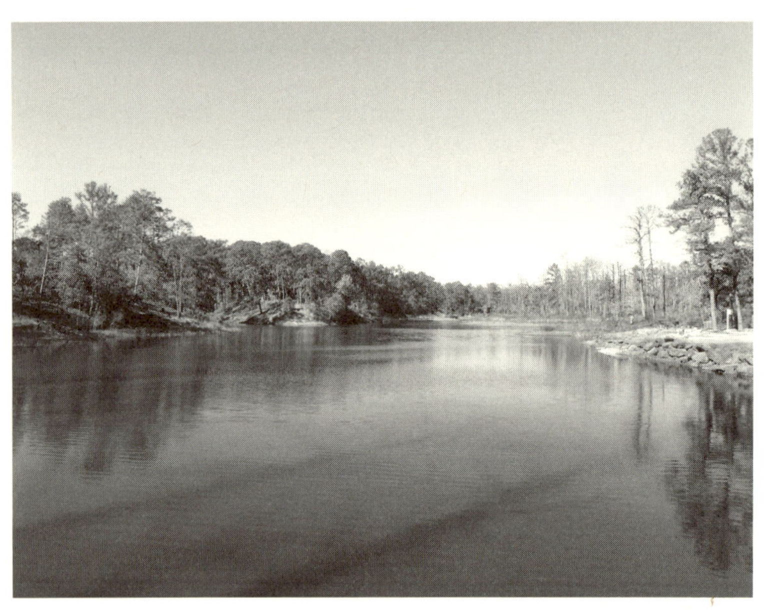

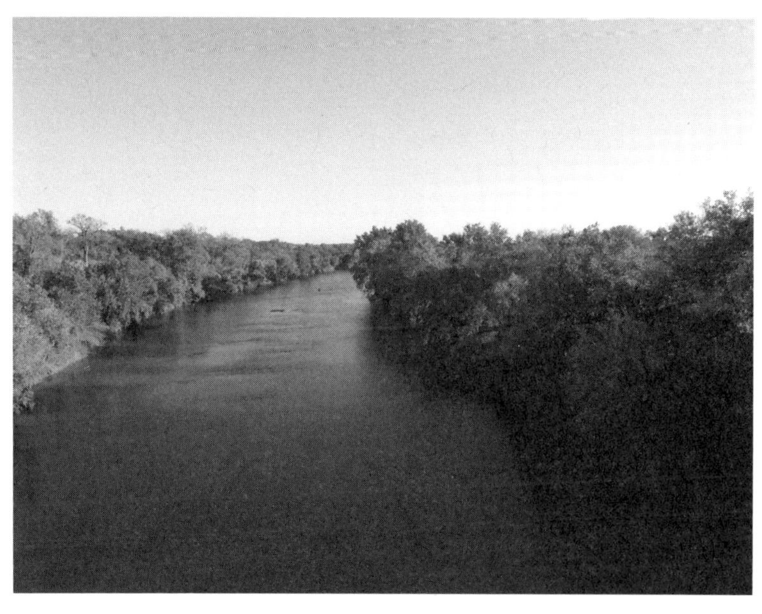

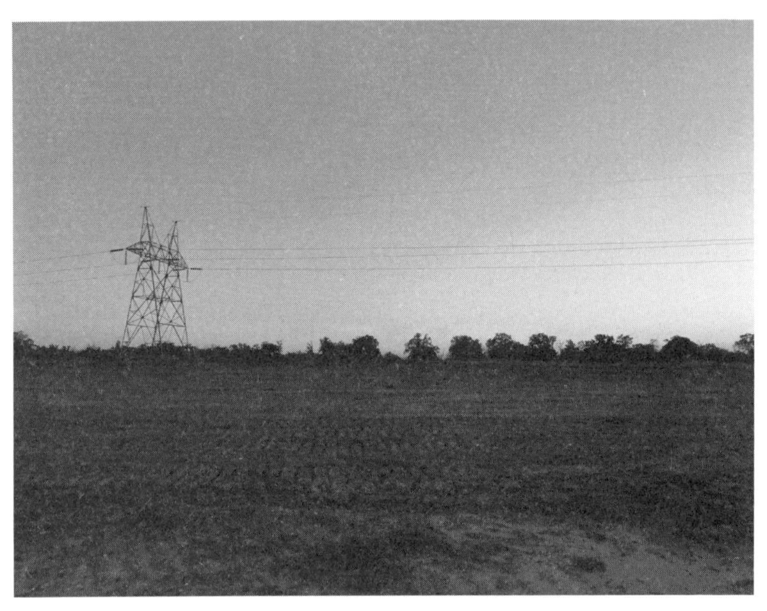

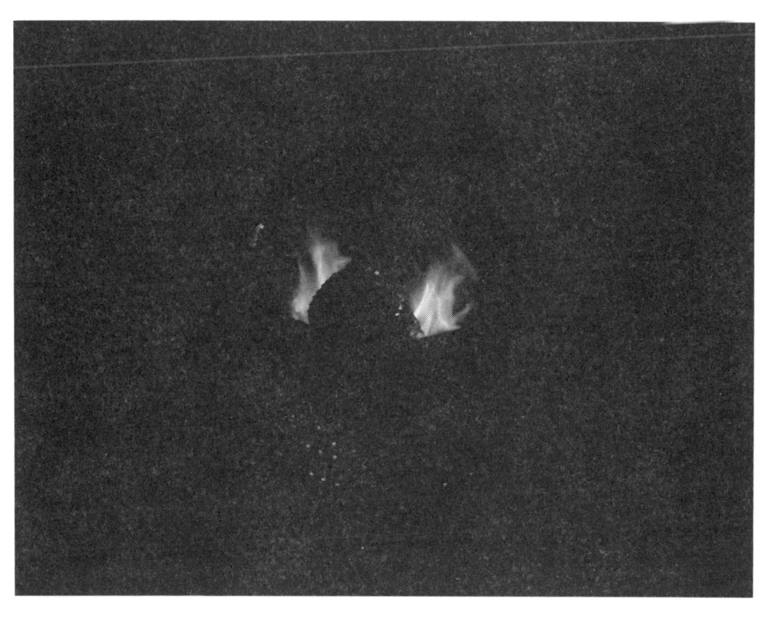

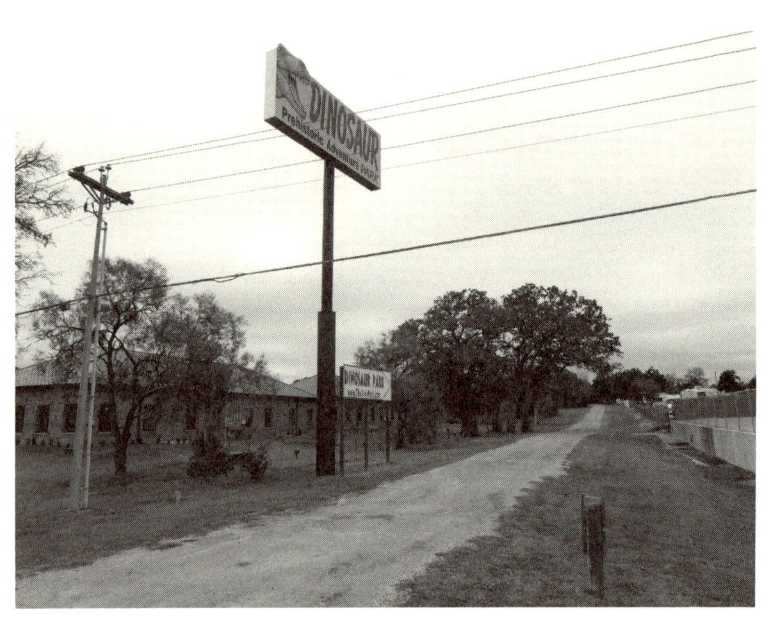
DINOSAUR
Prehistoric Adventure PARK
DINOSAUR PARK

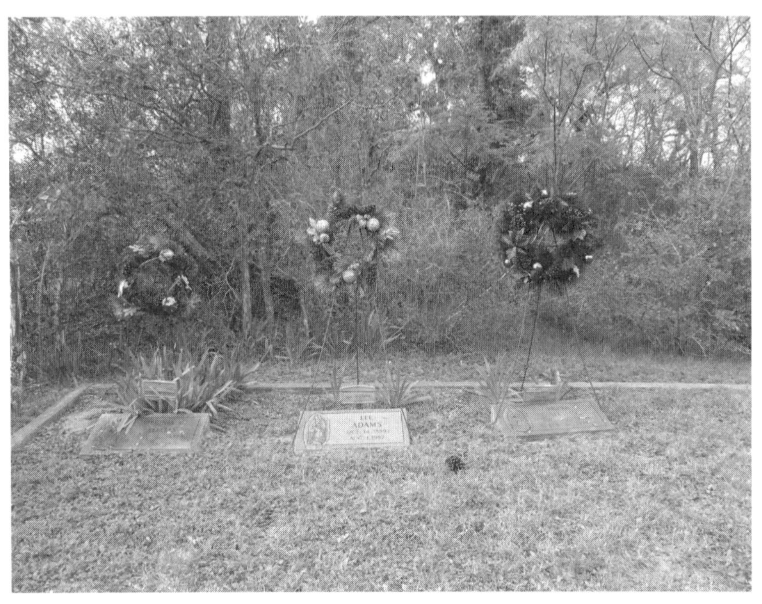
ADAMS

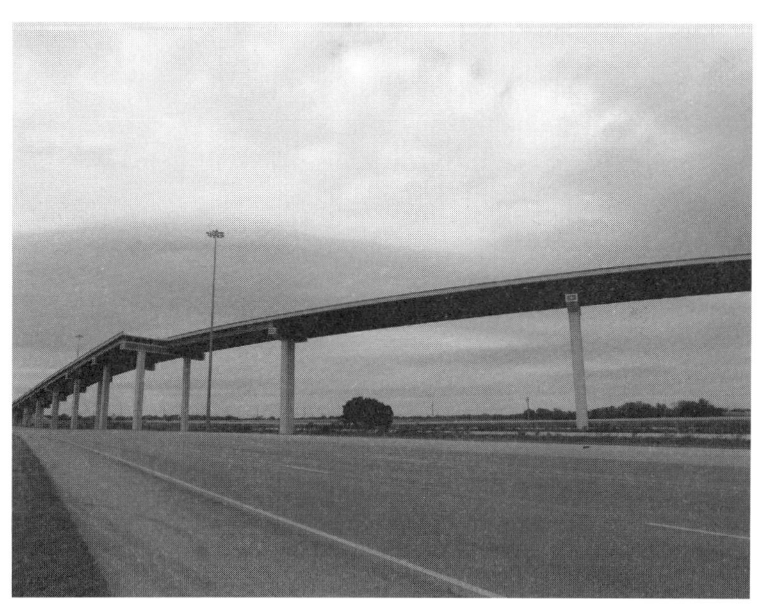

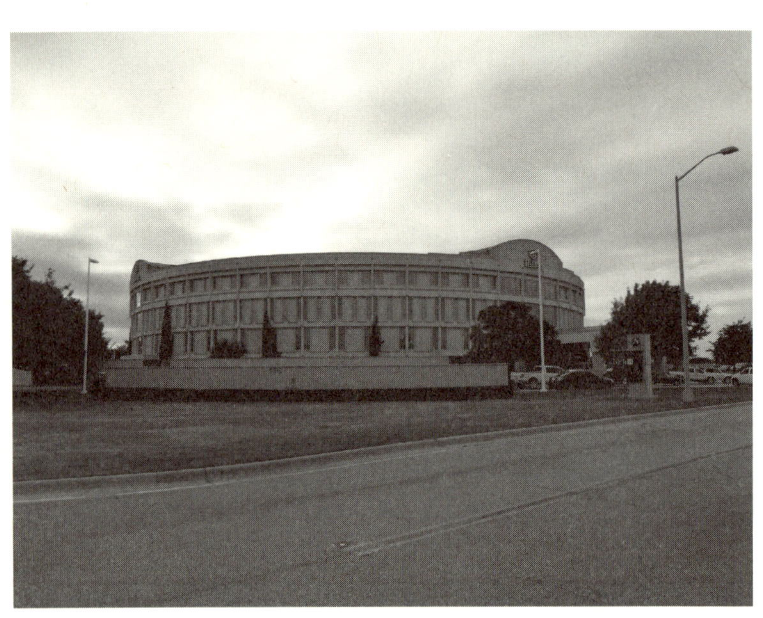

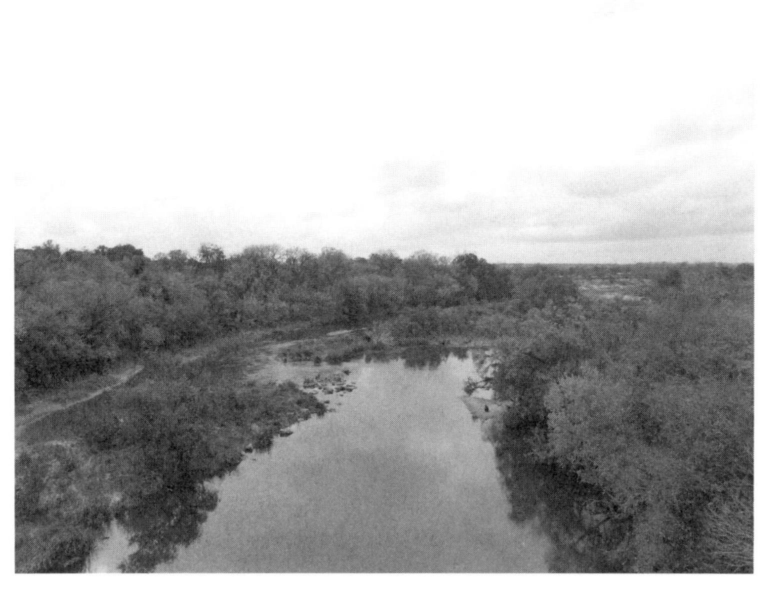

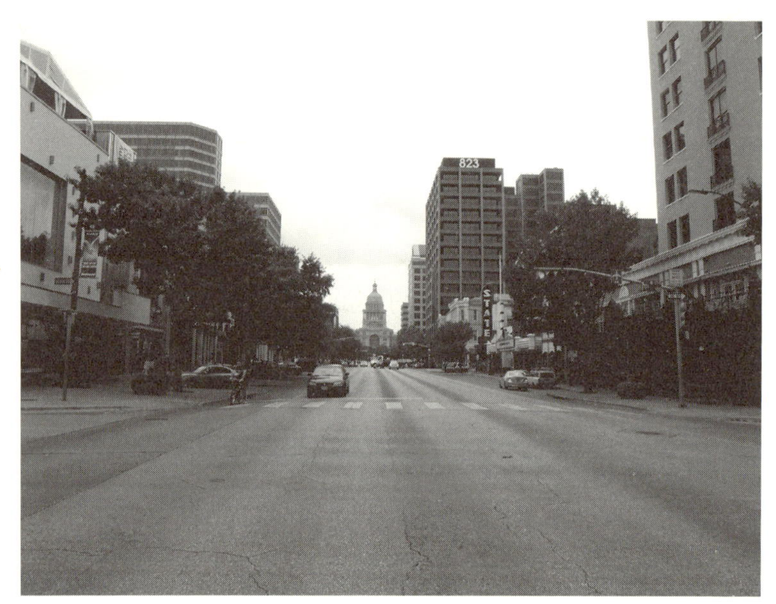
823
STATE

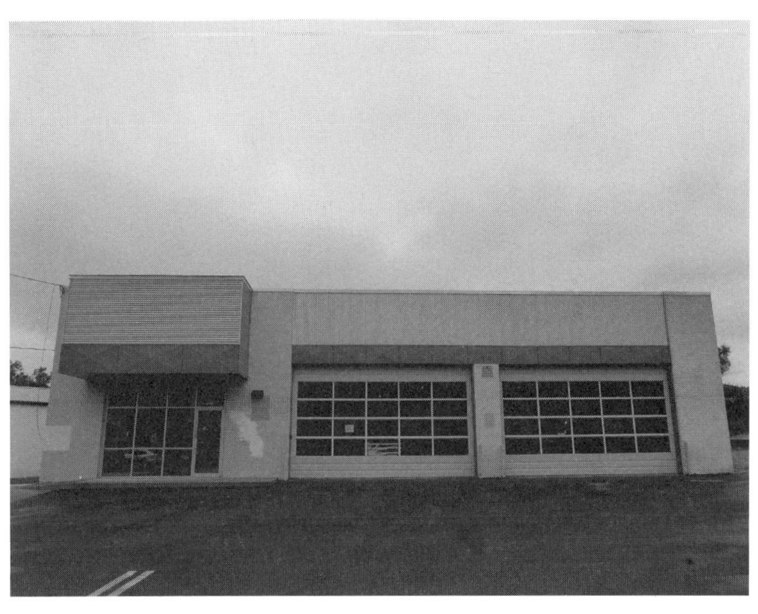

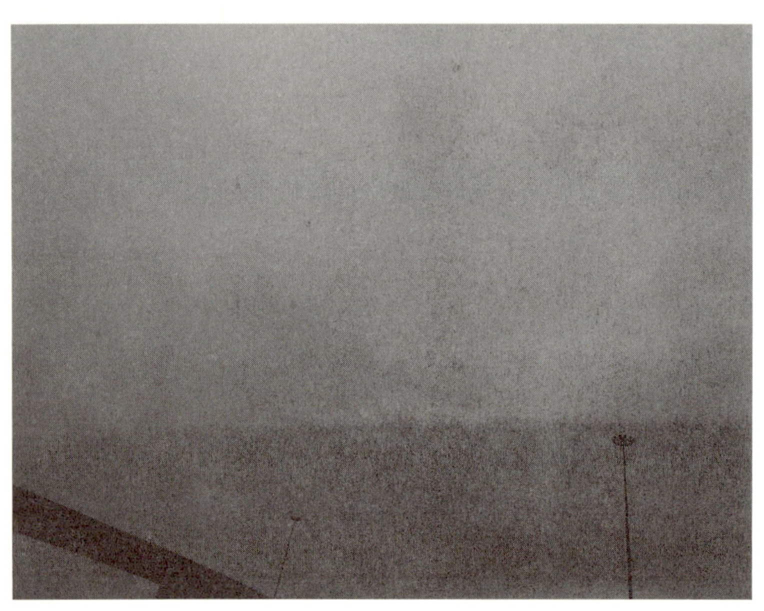

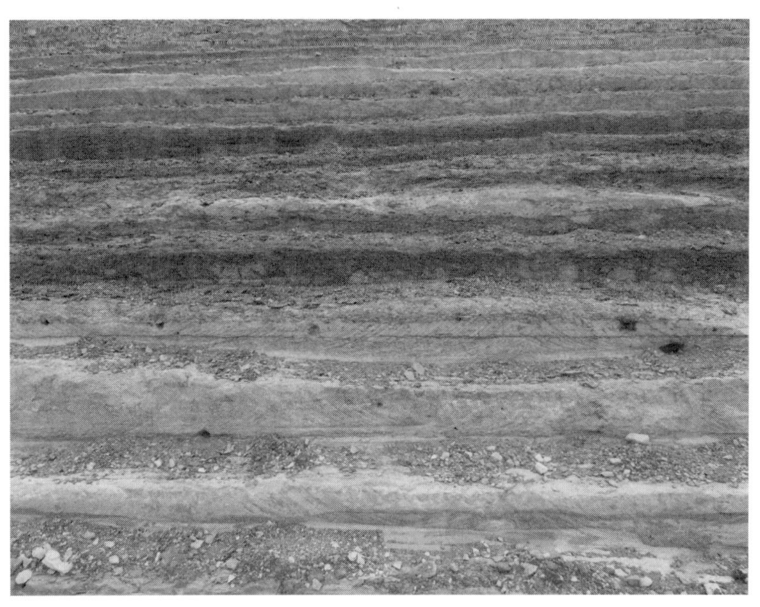

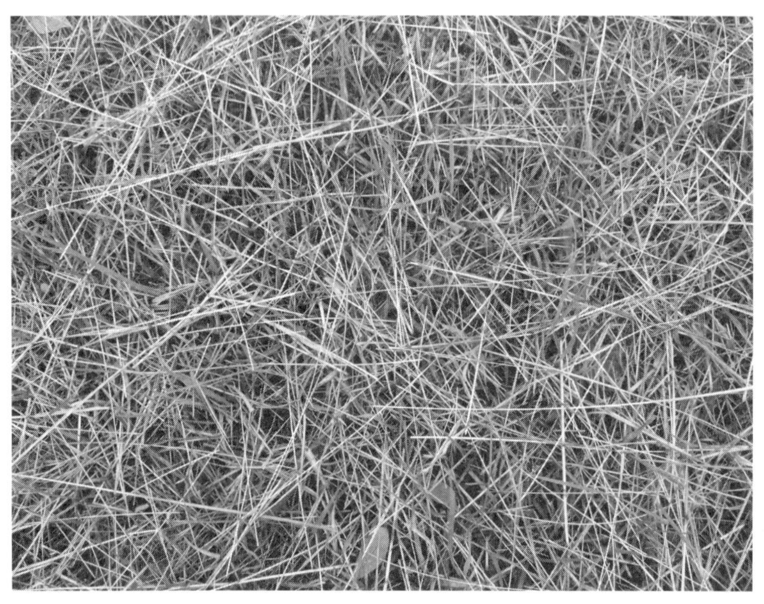

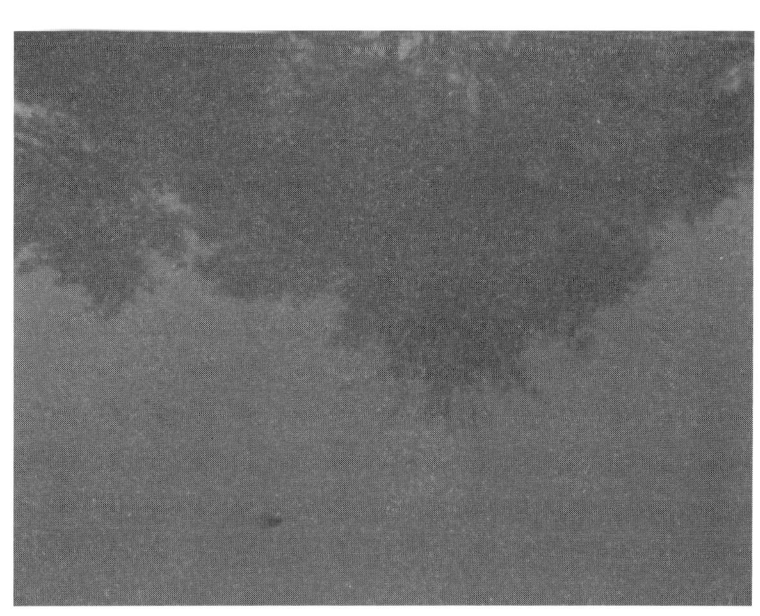

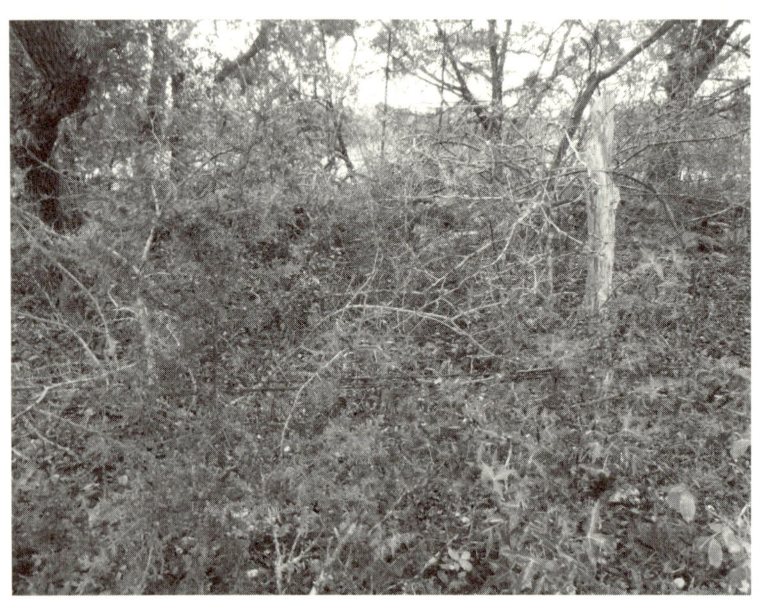

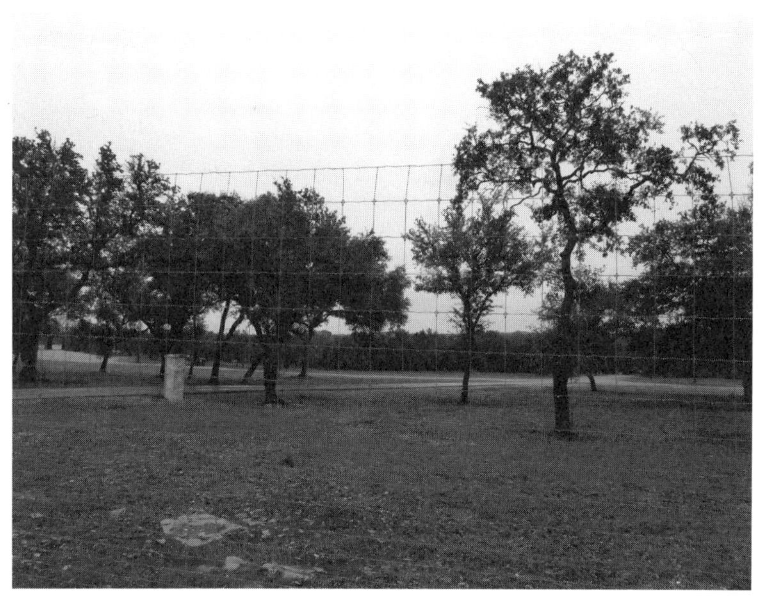

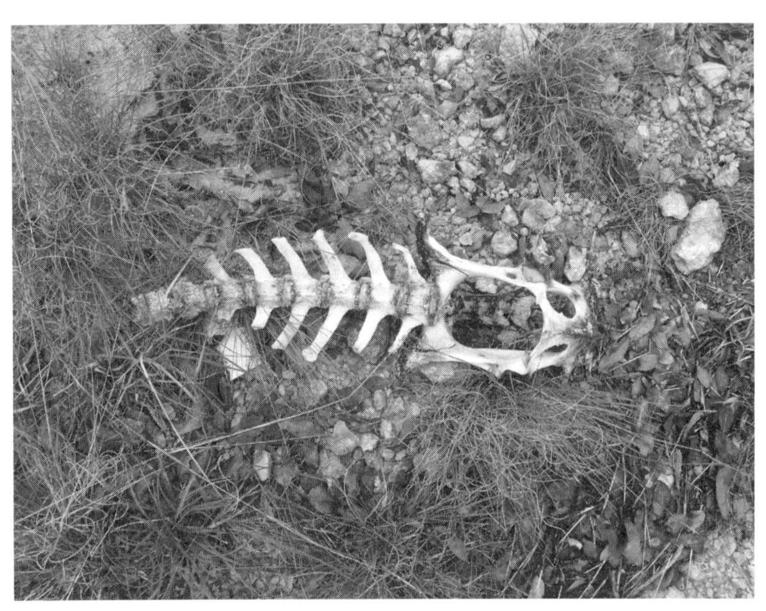

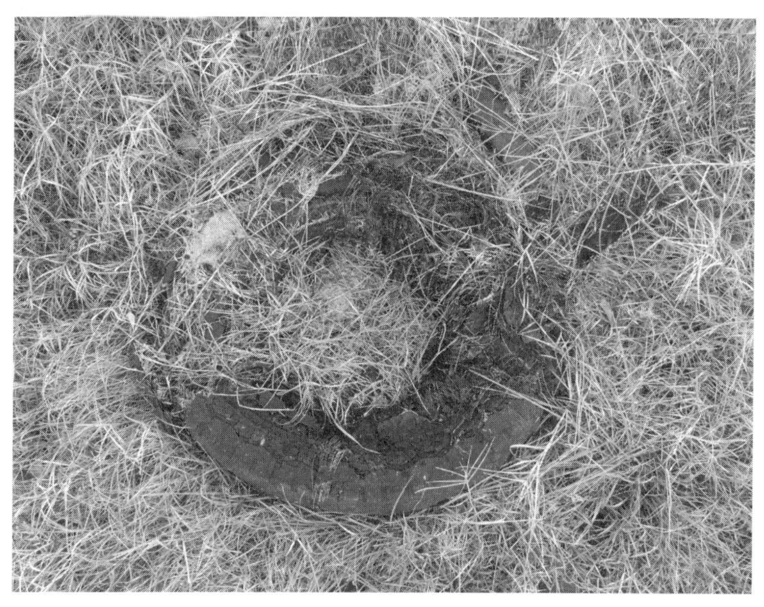

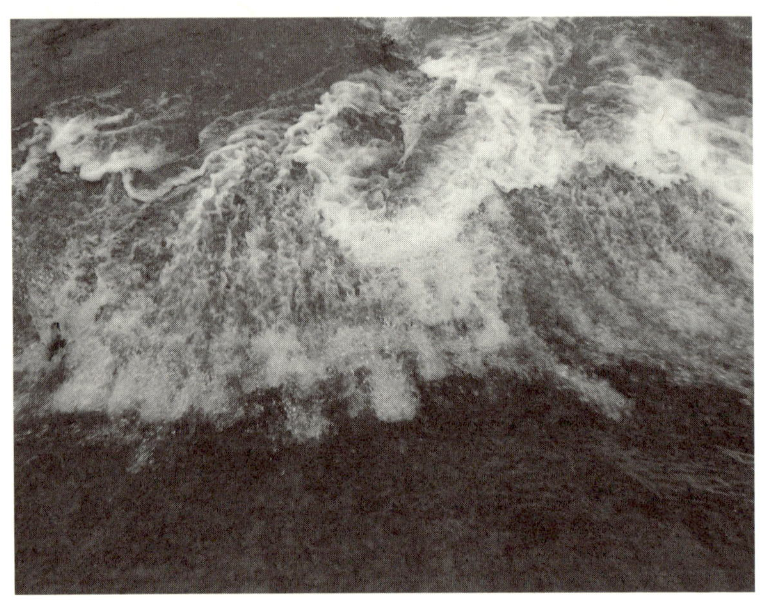

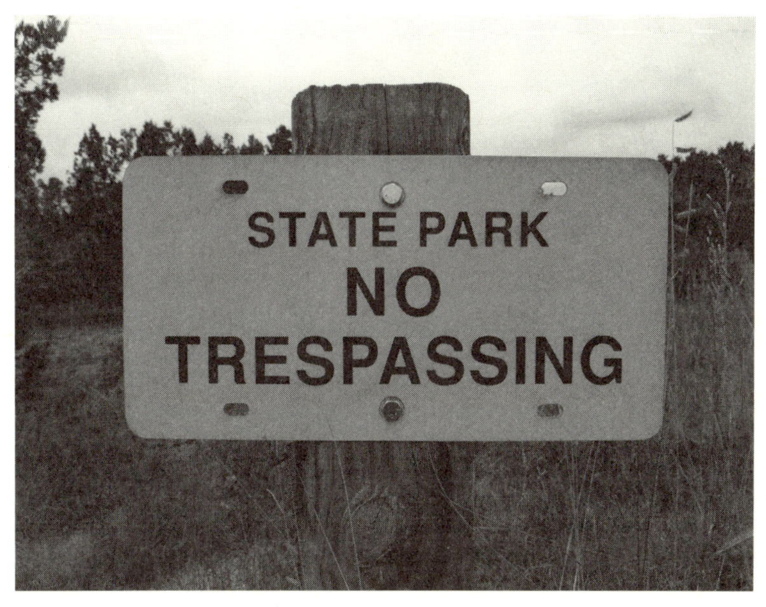
STATE PARK
NO
TRESPASSING

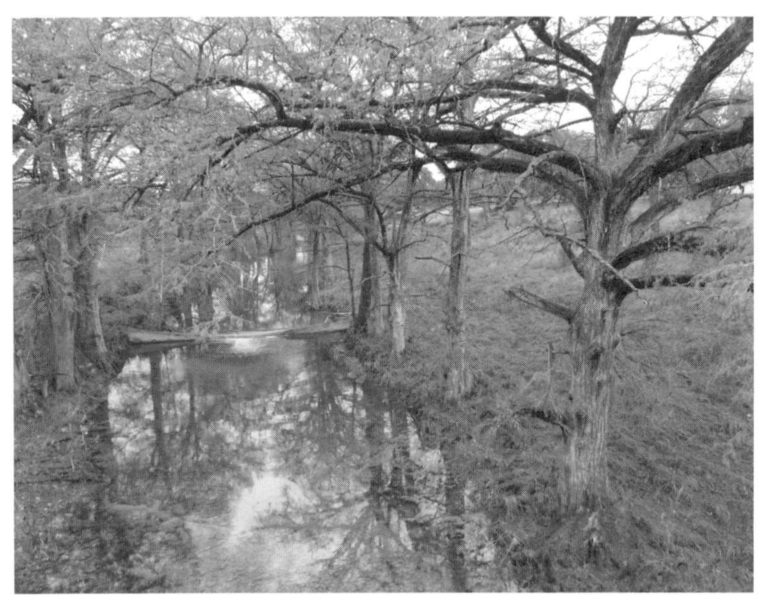

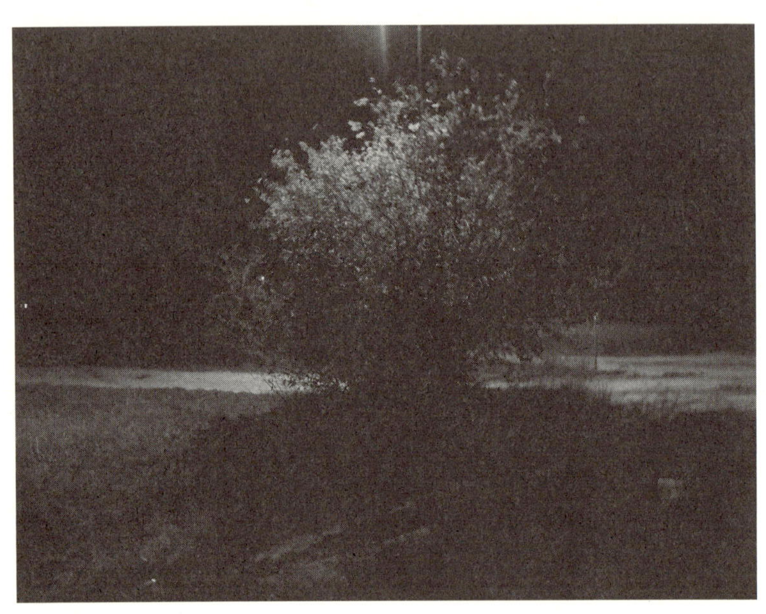

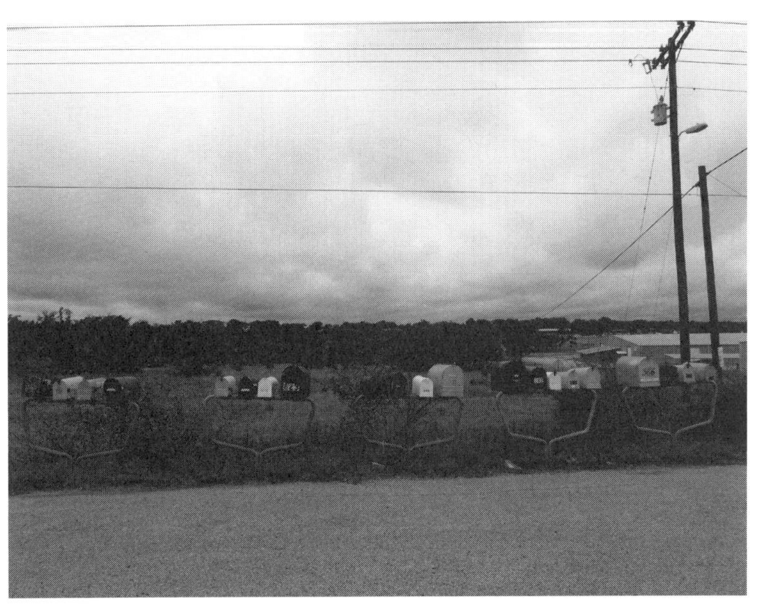

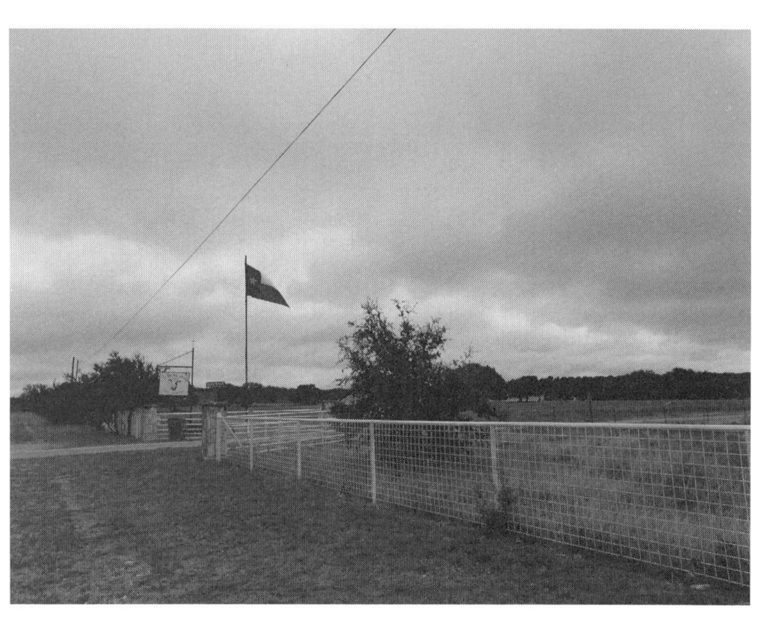

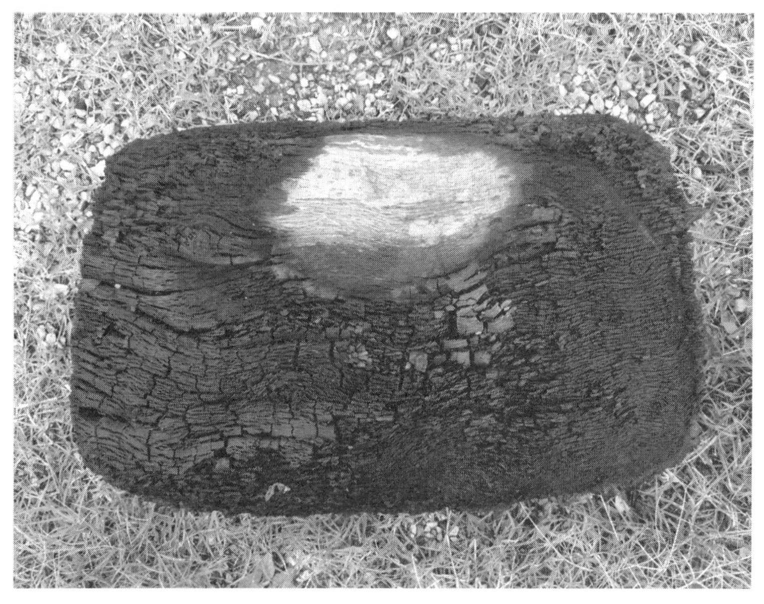

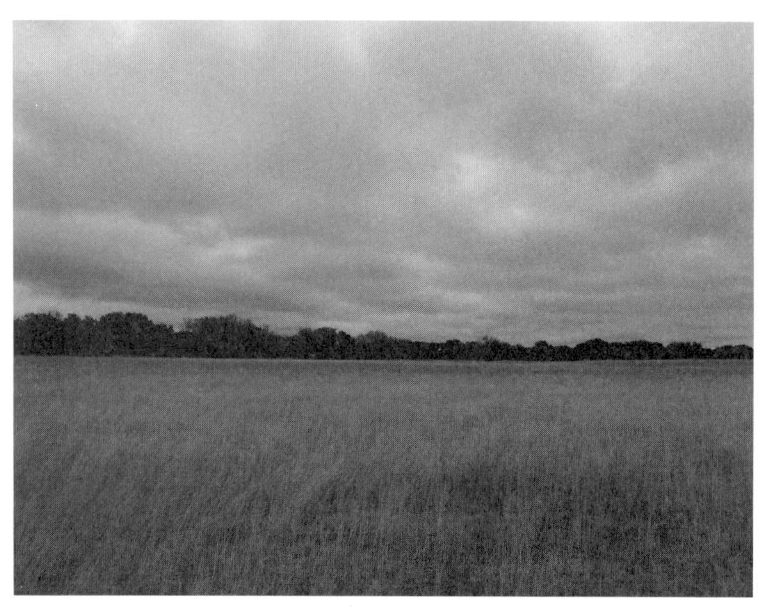

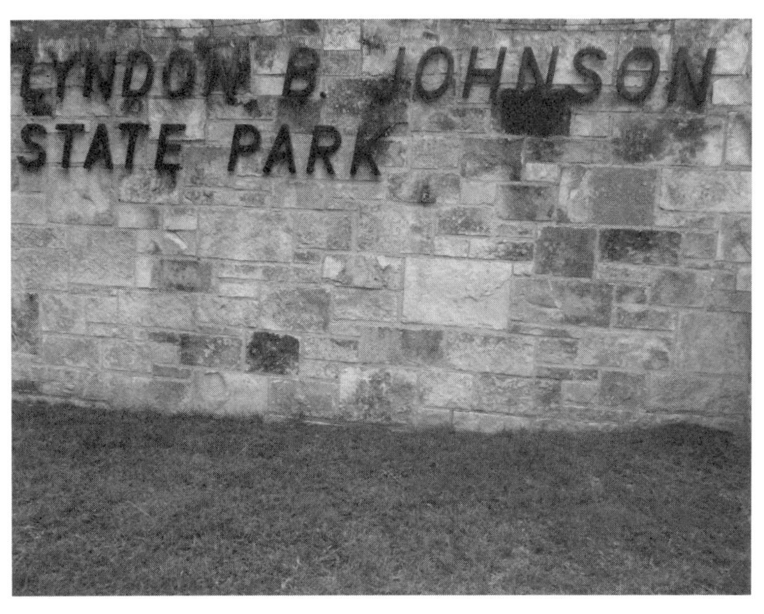
LYNDON B. JOHNSON
STATE PARK

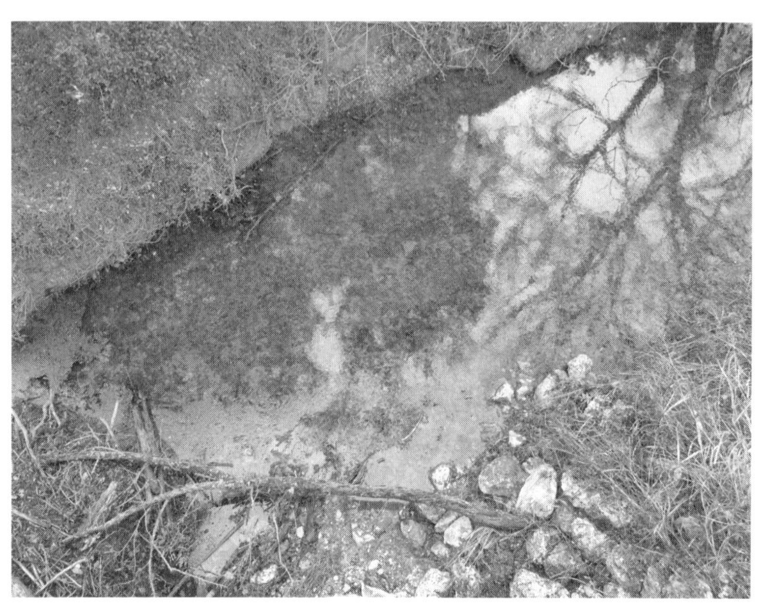

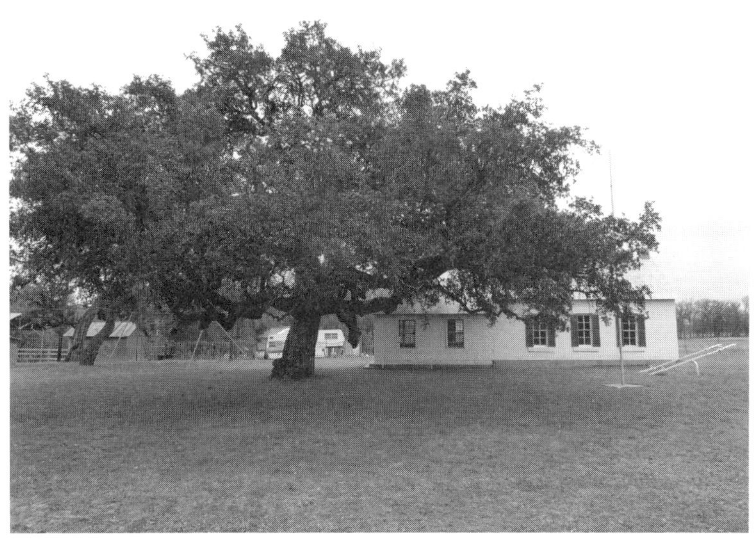

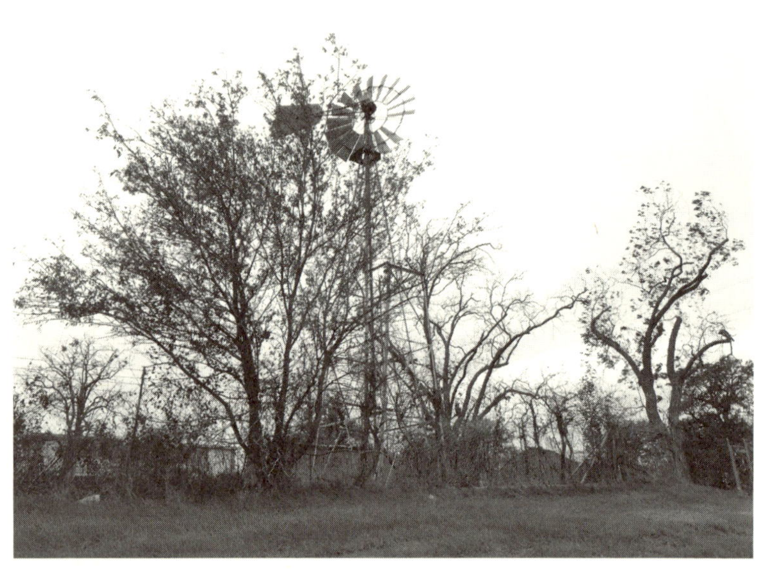

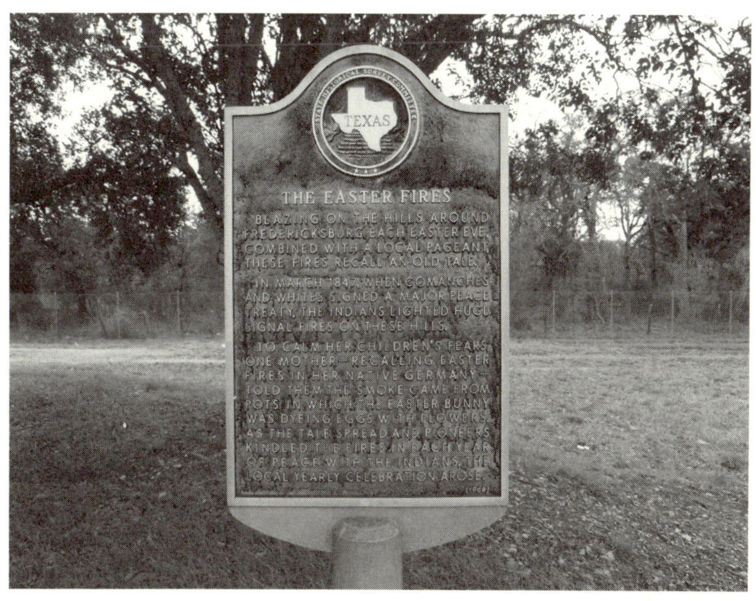
TEXAS
THE EASTER FIRES
BLAZING ON THE HILLS AROUND FREDERICKSBURG EACH EASTER EVE, COMBINED WITH A LOCAL PAGEANT, THESE FIRES RECALL AN OLD TALE.
IN MARCH 1847, WHEN COMANCHES AND WHITES SIGNED A MAJOR PEACE TREATY, THE INDIANS LIGHTED HUGE SIGNAL FIRES ON THESE HILLS.
TO CALM HER CHILDREN'S FEARS, ONE MOTHER—RECALLING EASTER FIRES IN HER NATIVE GERMANY—TOLD THEM THE SMOKE CAME FROM POTS IN WHICH THE EASTER BUNNY WAS DYEING EGGS WITH FLOWERS.
AS THE TALE SPREAD AND PIONEERS KINDLED THE FIRES IN EACH YEAR OF PEACE WITH THE INDIANS, THE LOCAL YEARLY CELEBRATION AROSE.

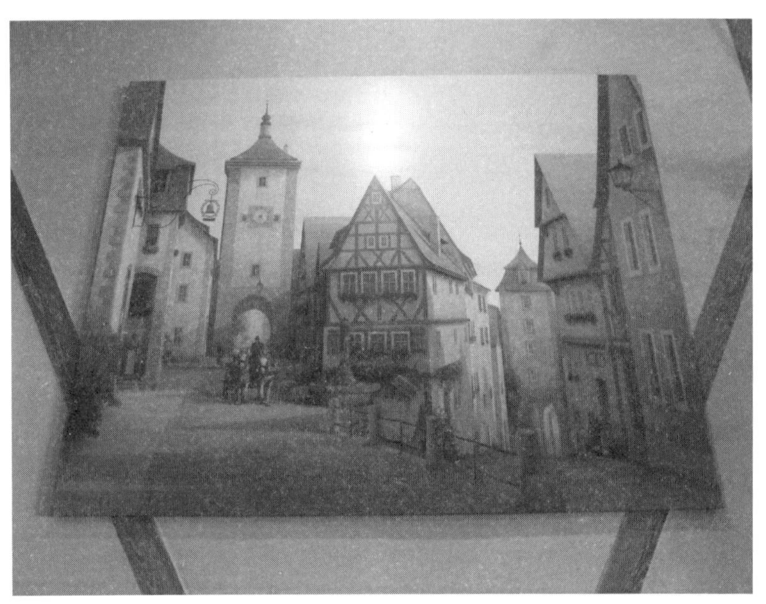

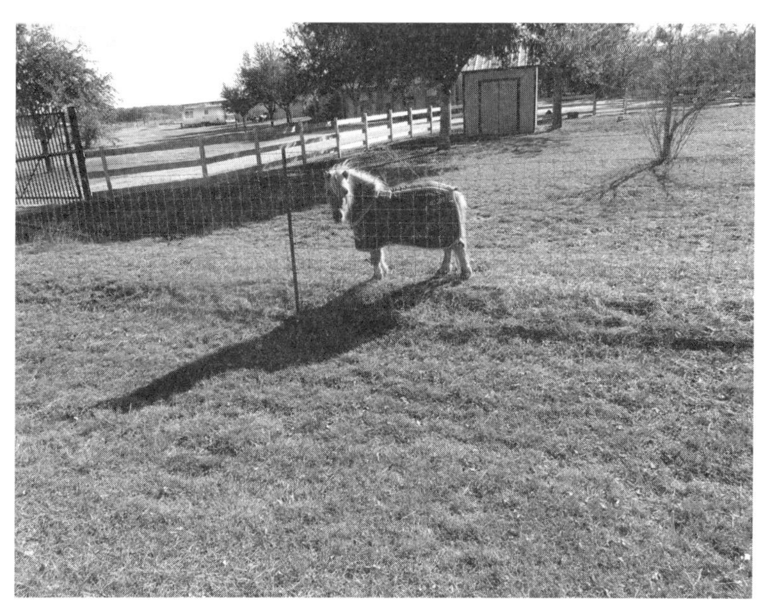

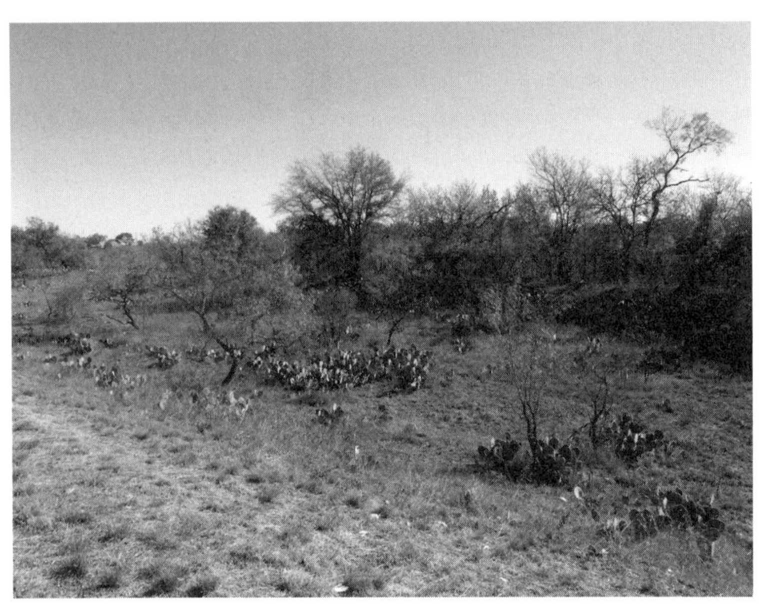

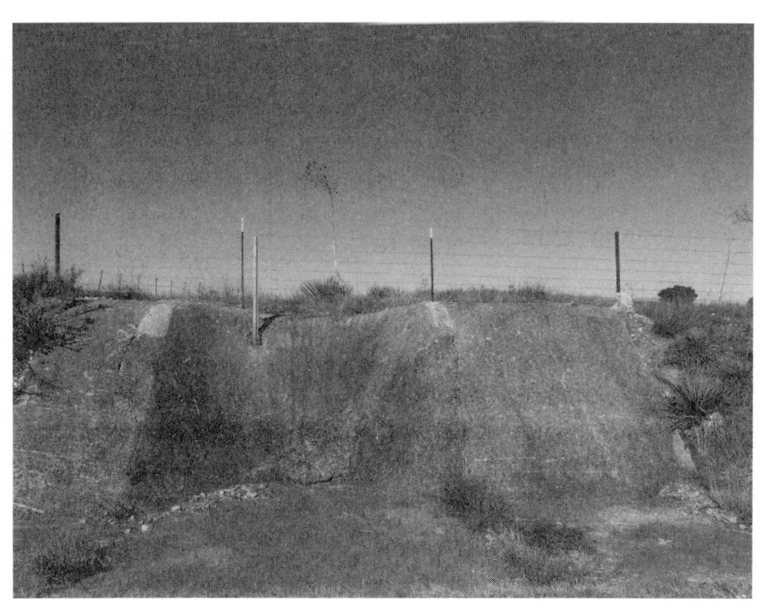

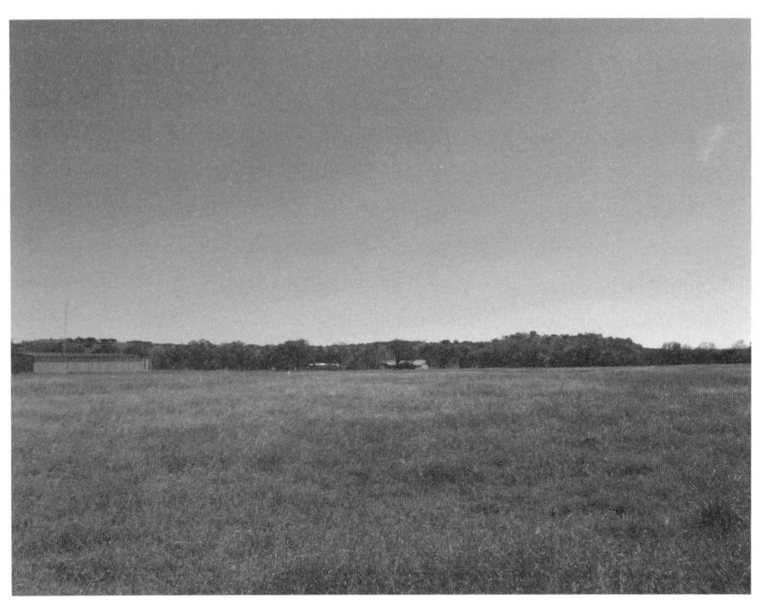

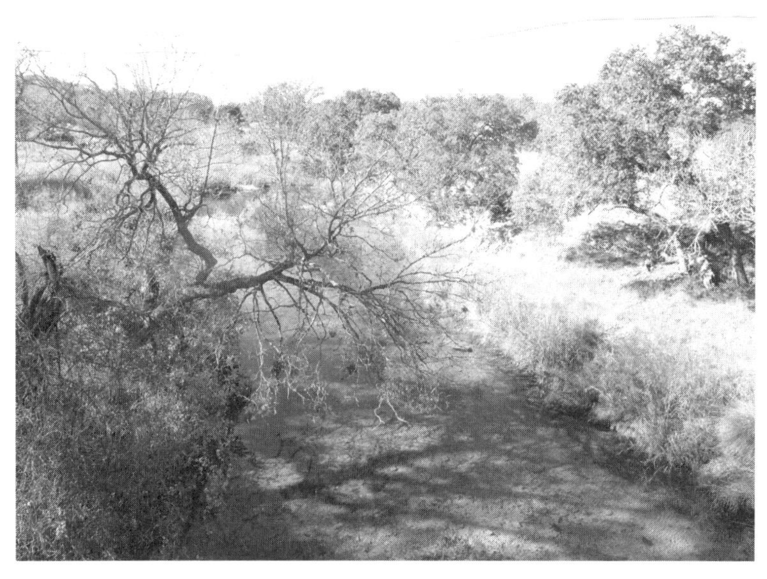

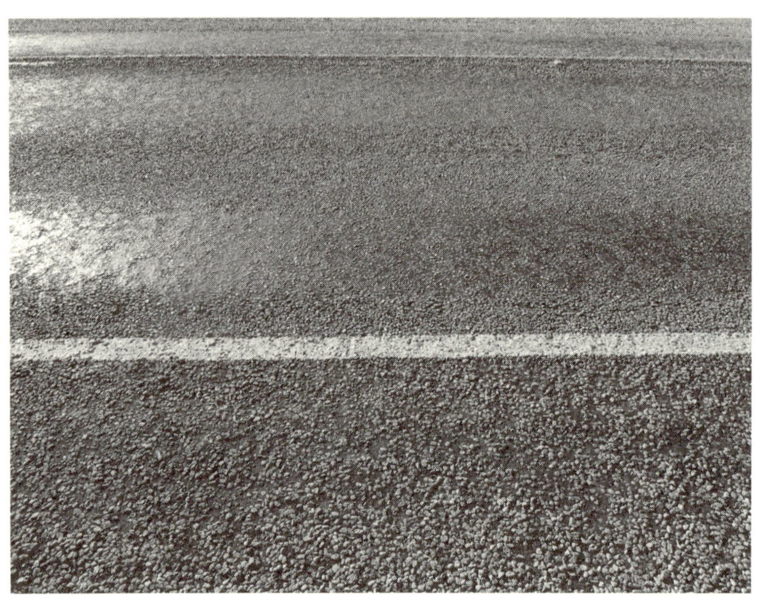

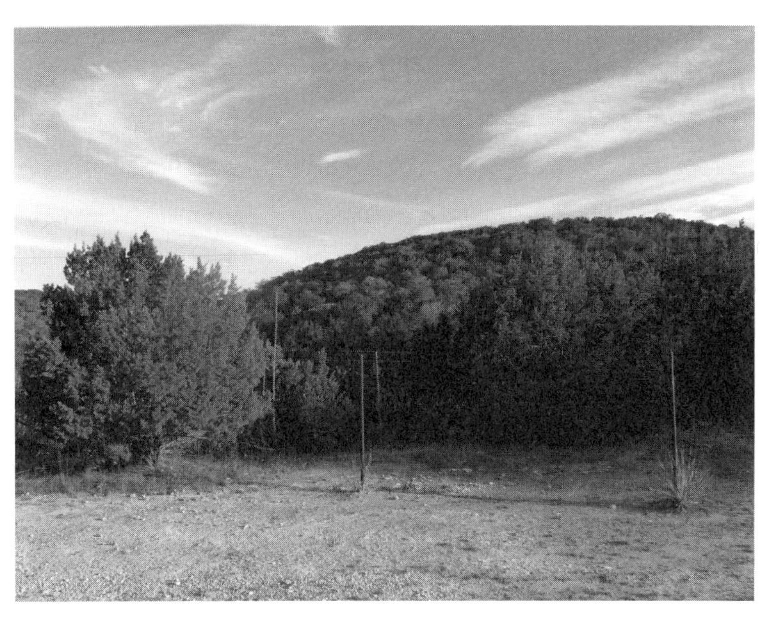

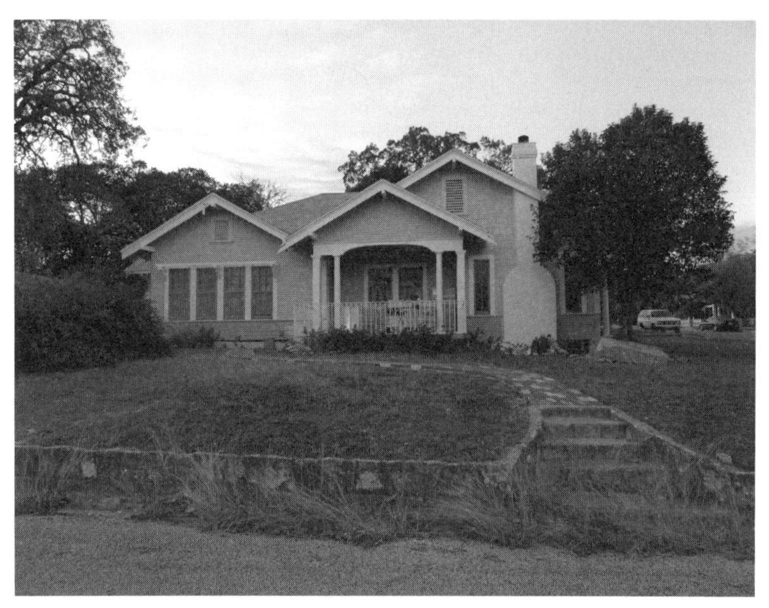

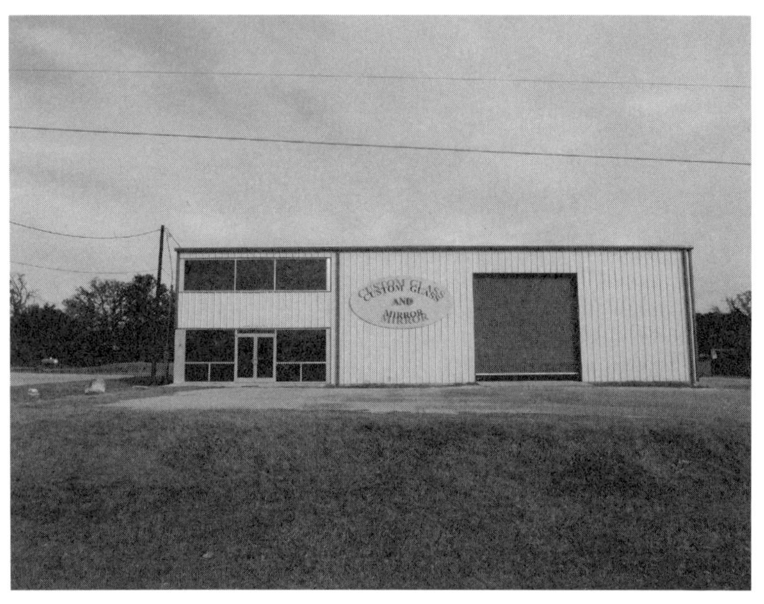
CUSTOM GLASS
AND
MIRROR

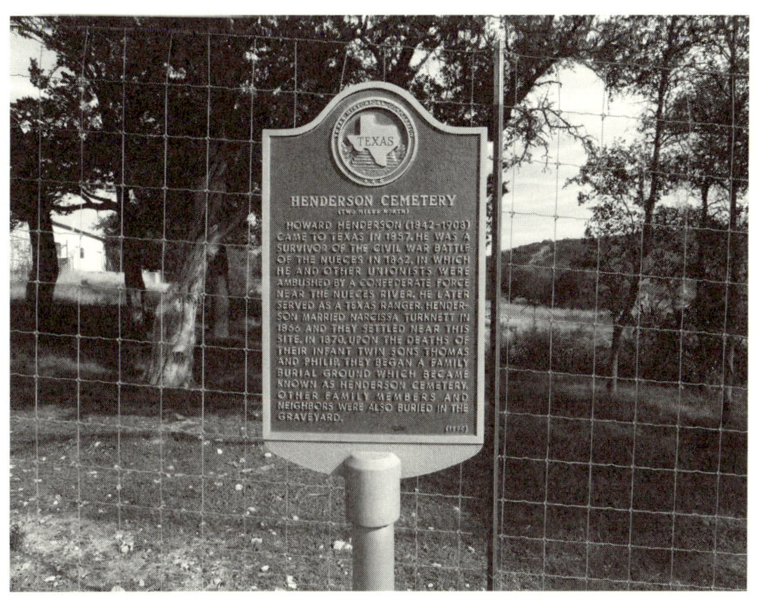
TEXAS
HENDERSON CEMETERY
HOWARD HENDERSON (1842–1908) CAME TO TEXAS IN 1857. HE WAS A SURVIVOR OF THE CIVIL WAR BATTLE OF THE NUECES IN 1862, IN WHICH HE AND OTHER UNIONISTS WERE AMBUSHED BY A CONFEDERATE FORCE NEAR THE NUECES RIVER. HE LATER SERVED AS A TEXAS RANGER. HENDERSON MARRIED NARCISSA TURKNETT IN 1866 AND THEY SETTLED NEAR THIS SITE. IN 1870, UPON THE DEATHS OF THEIR INFANT TWIN SONS THOMAS AND PHILIP, THEY BEGAN A FAMILY BURIAL GROUND WHICH BECAME KNOWN AS HENDERSON CEMETERY. OTHER FAMILY MEMBERS AND NEIGHBORS WERE ALSO BURIED IN THE GRAVEYARD.

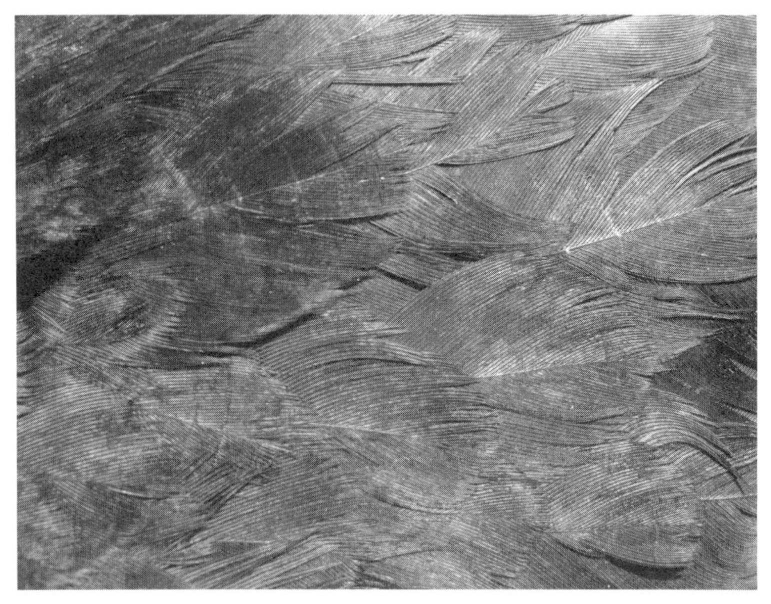

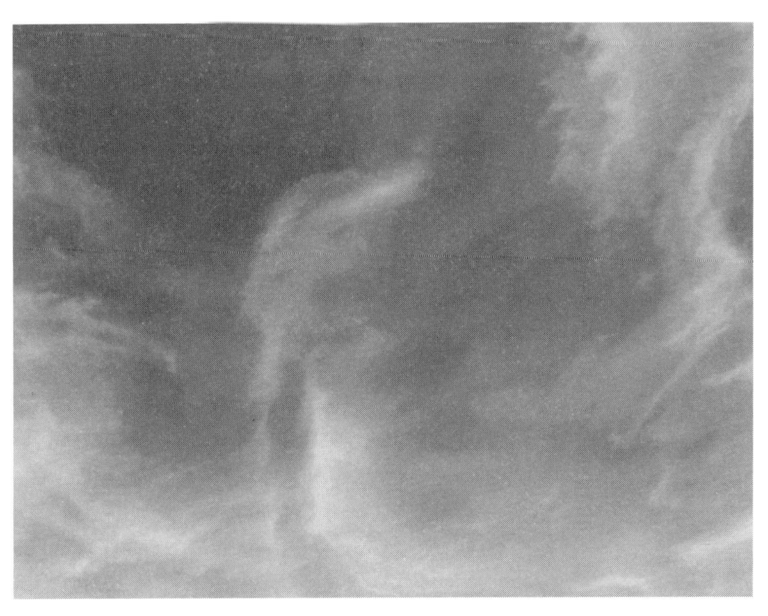

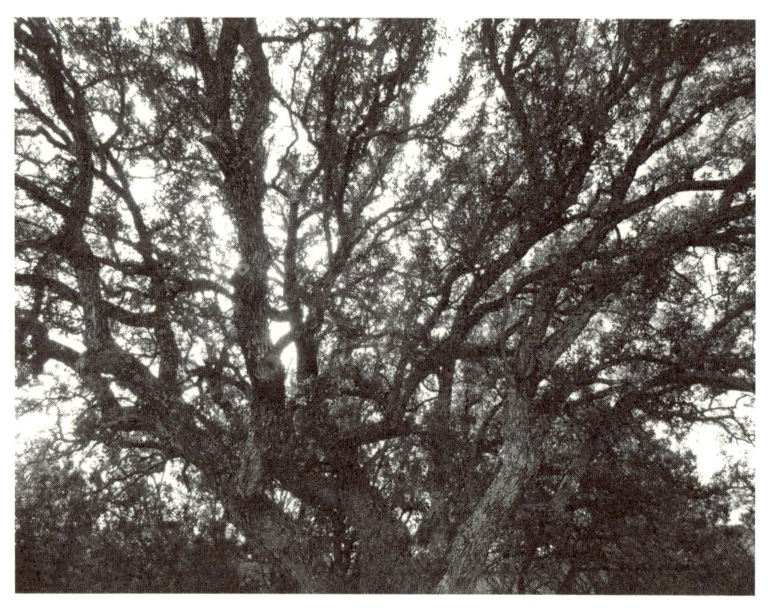

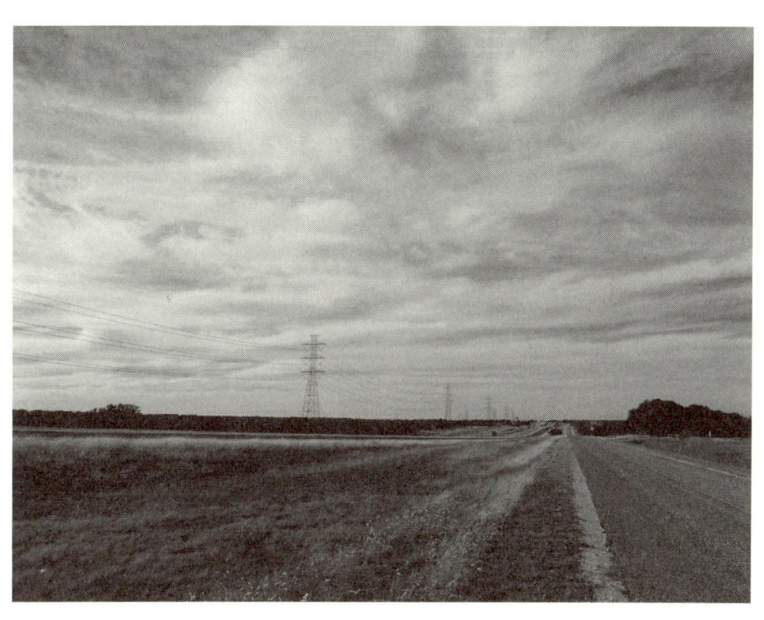

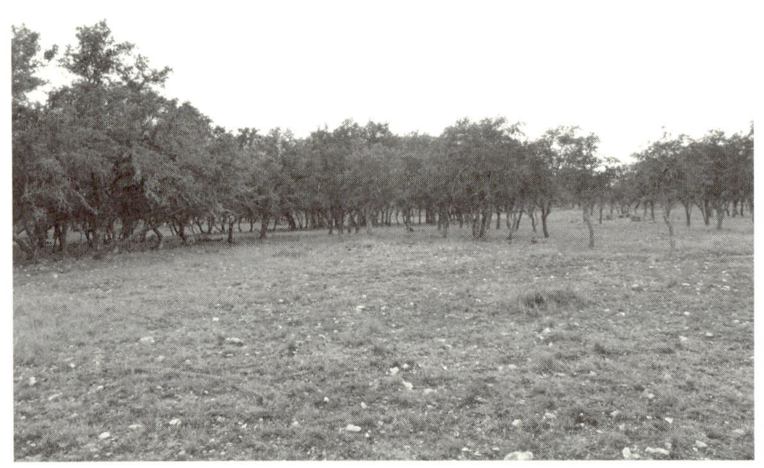

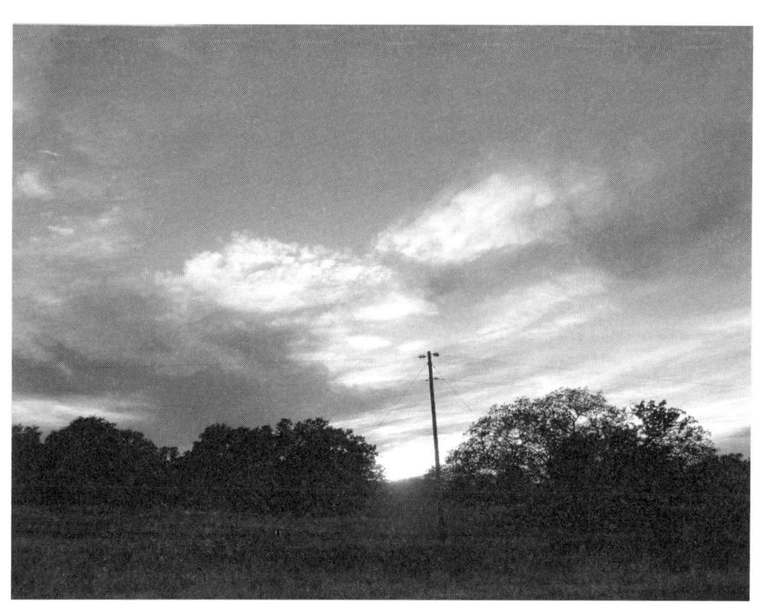

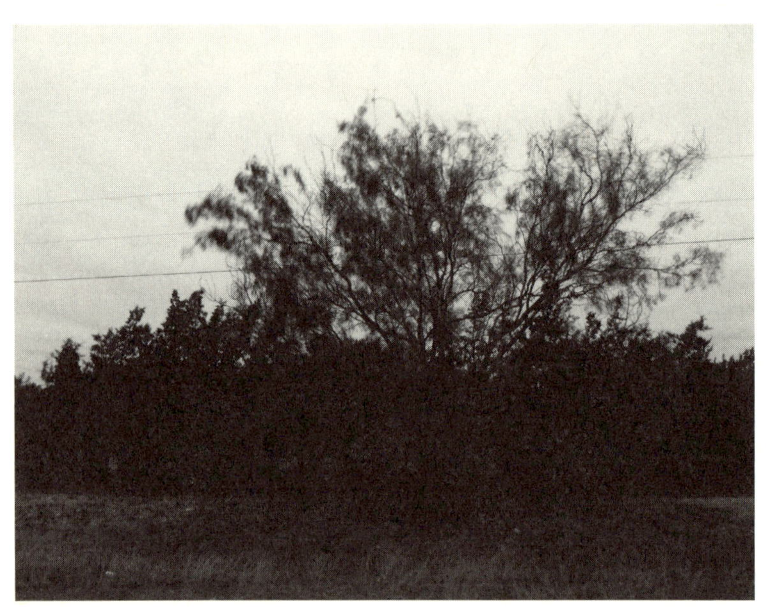

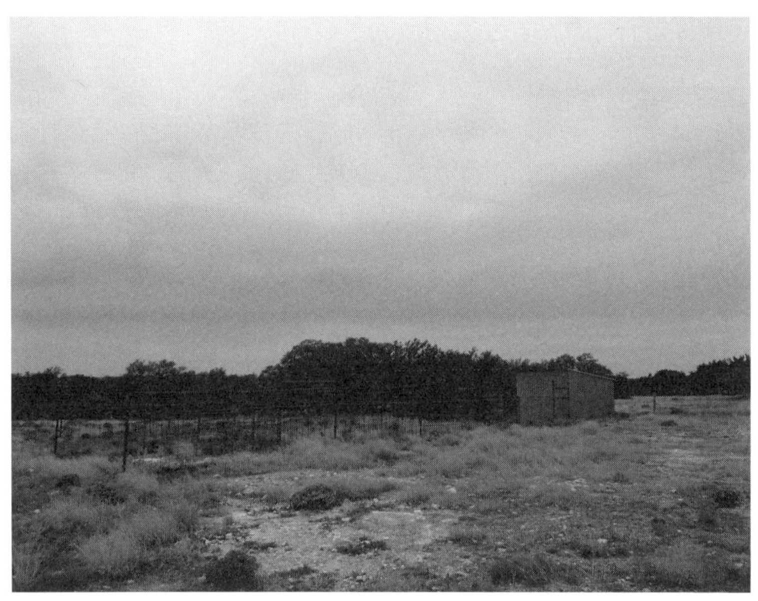

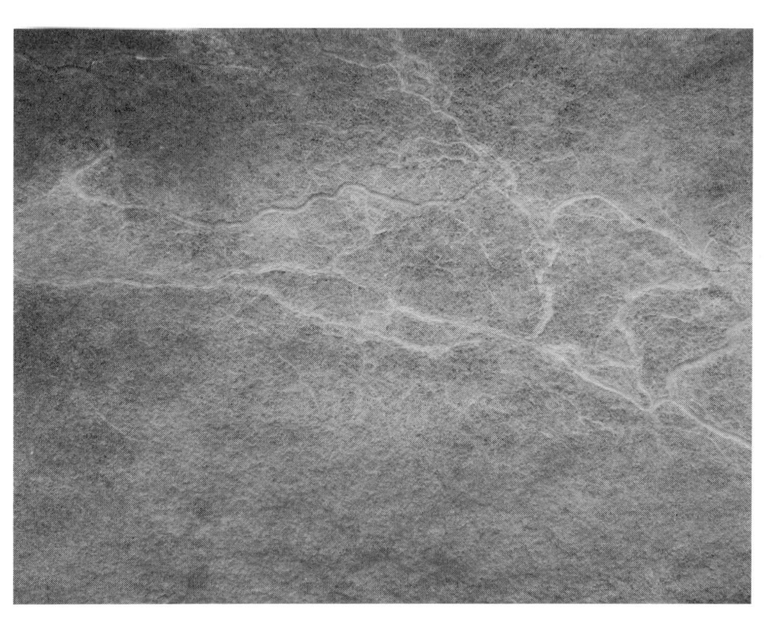

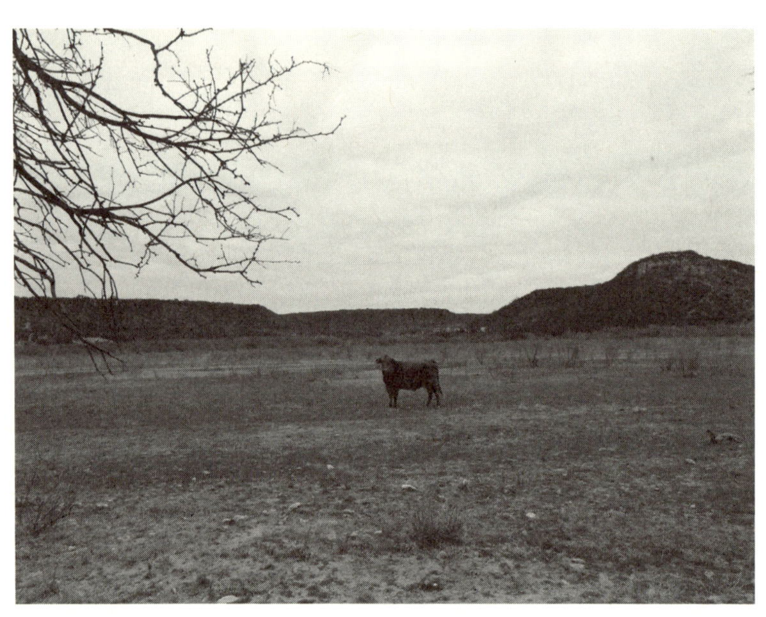

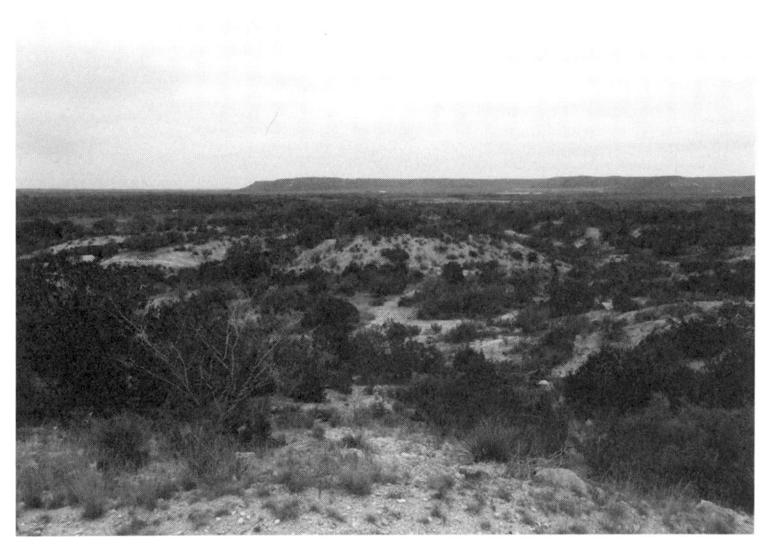

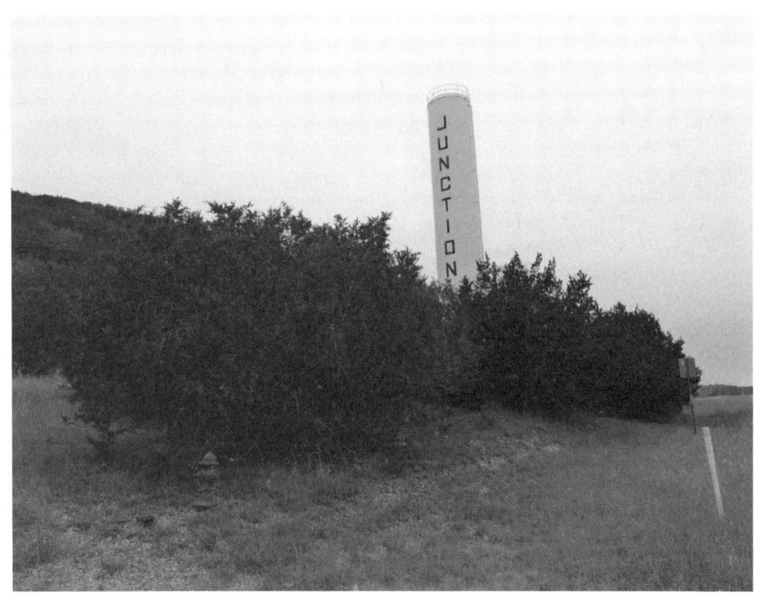
JUNCTION

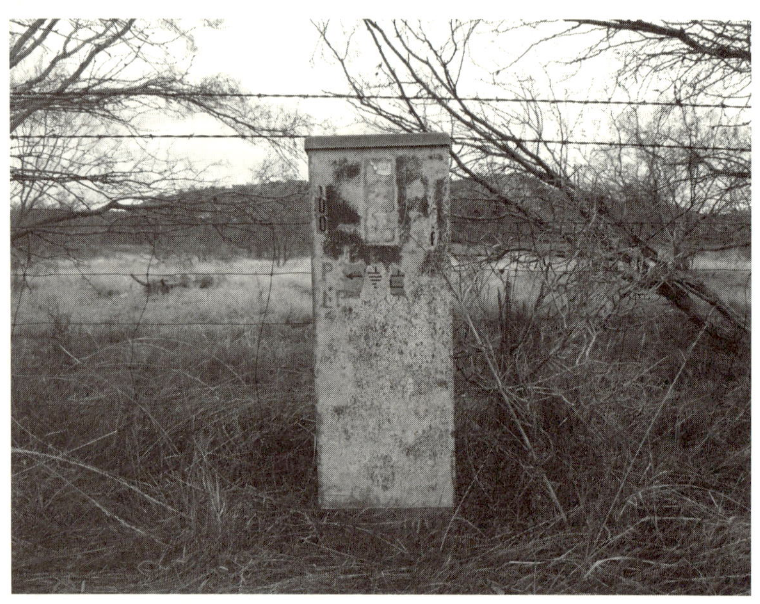

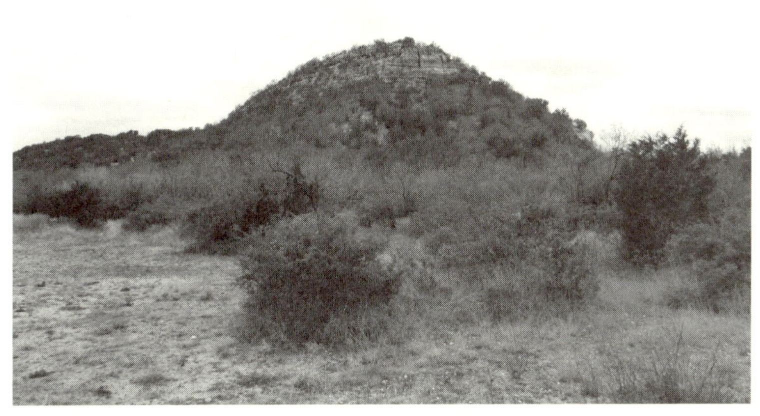

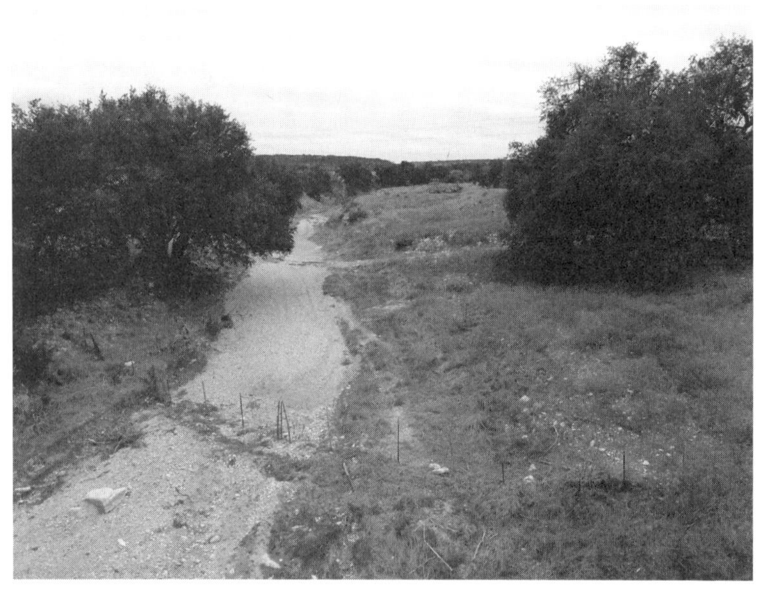

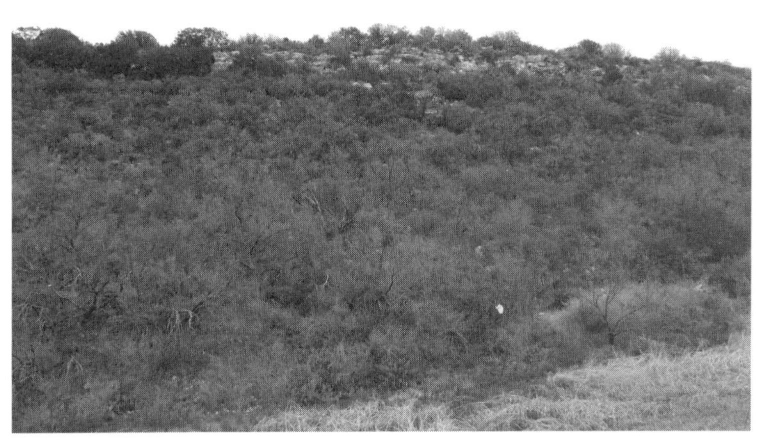

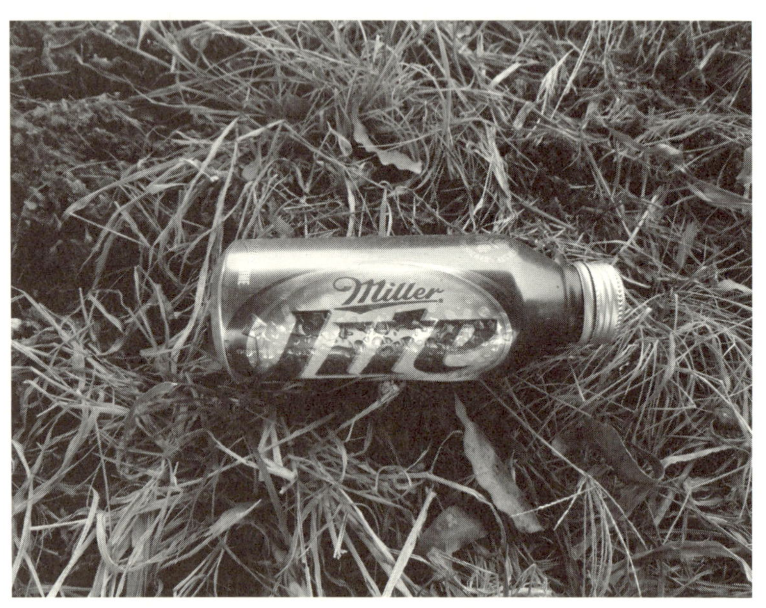
Miller
Lite

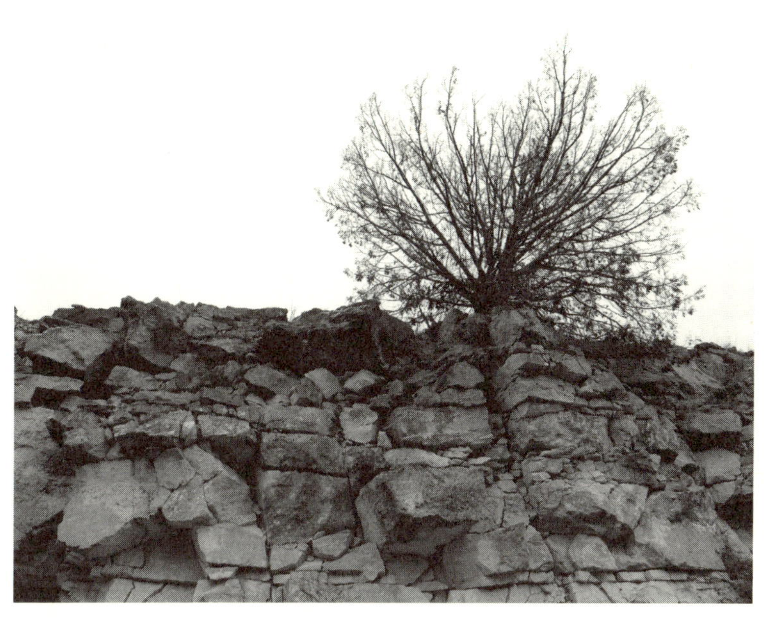

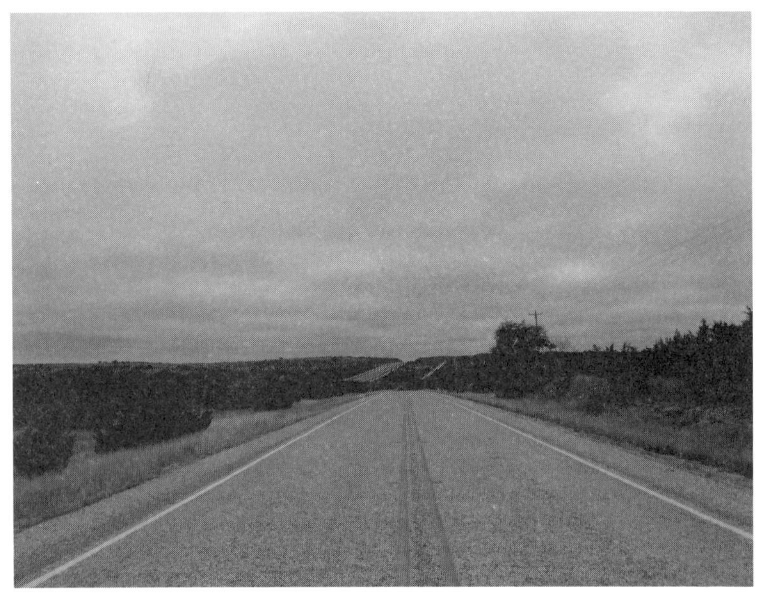

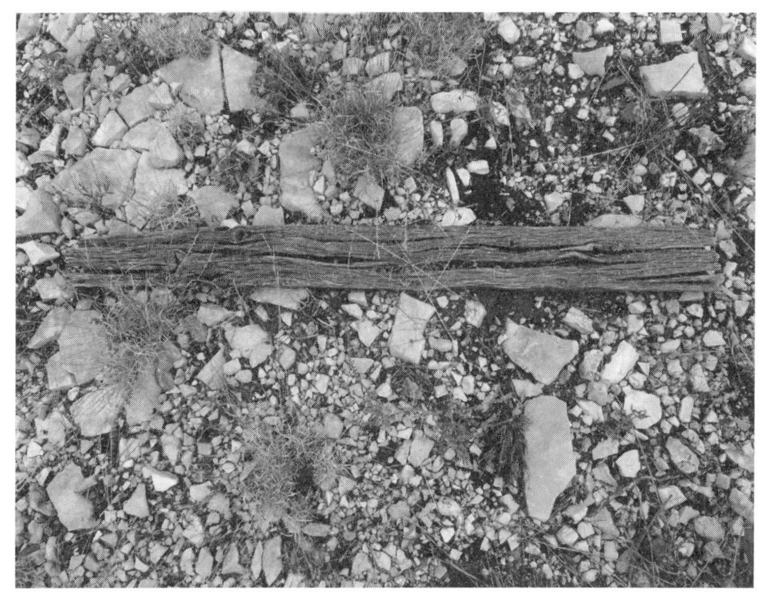

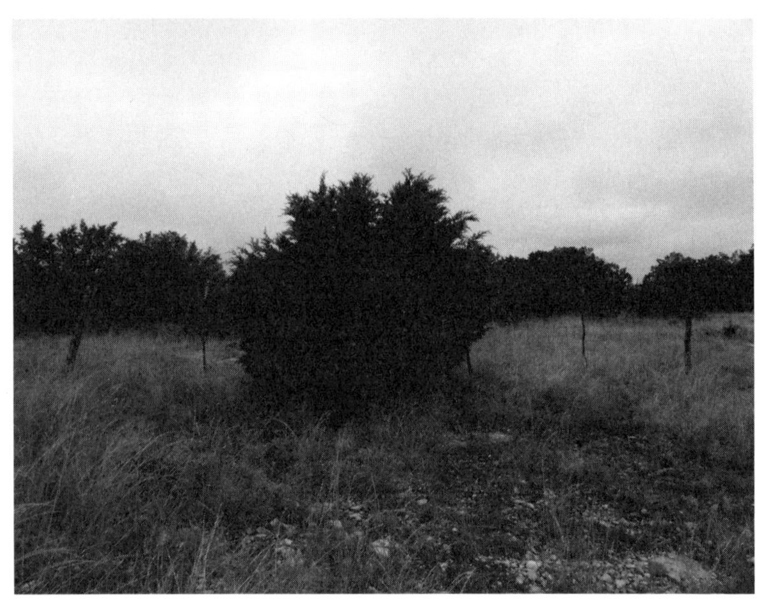

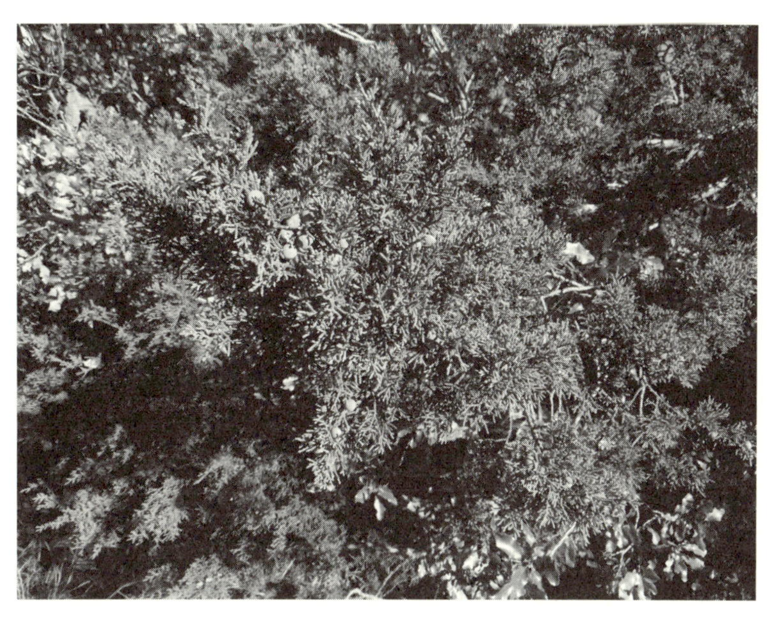

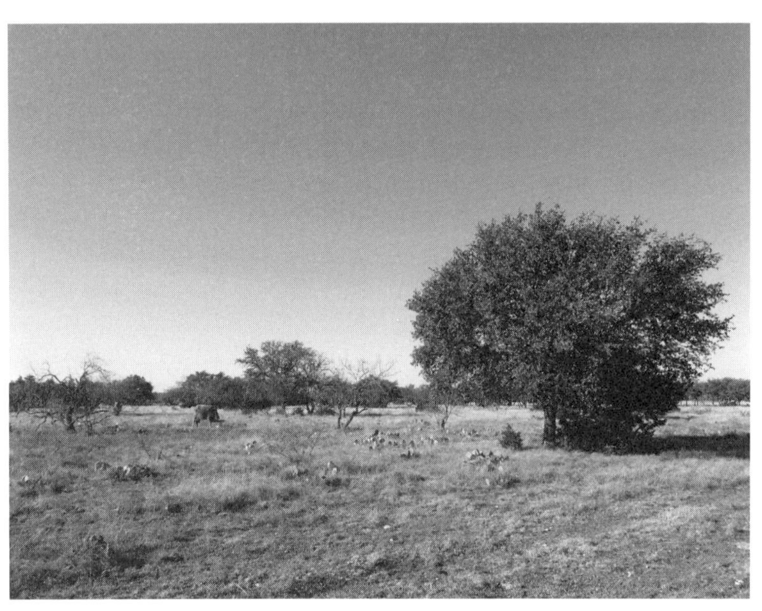

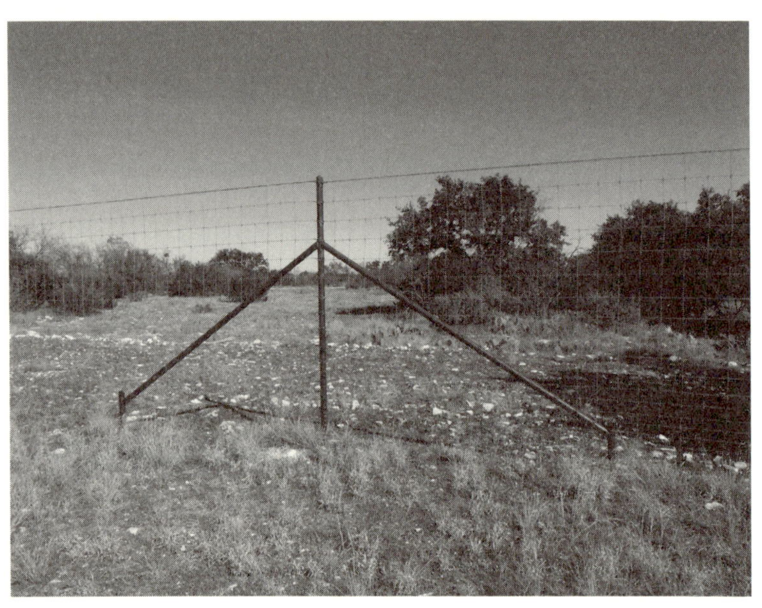

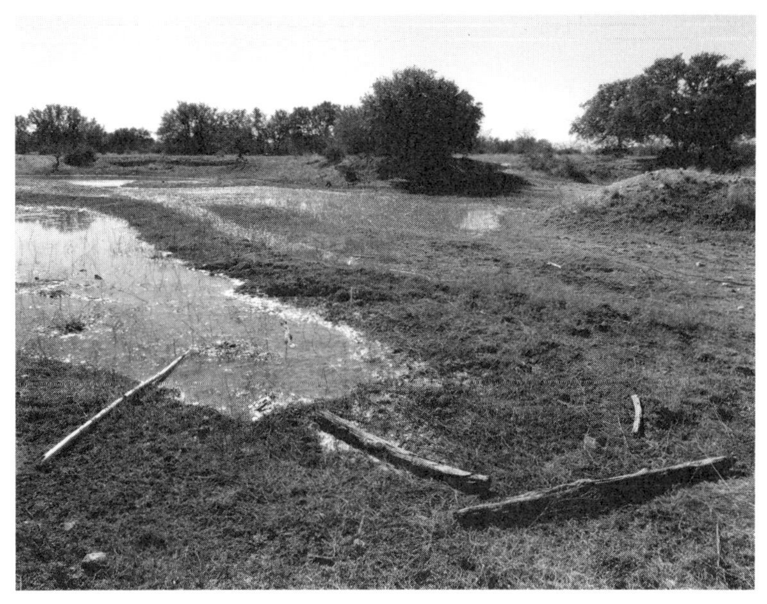

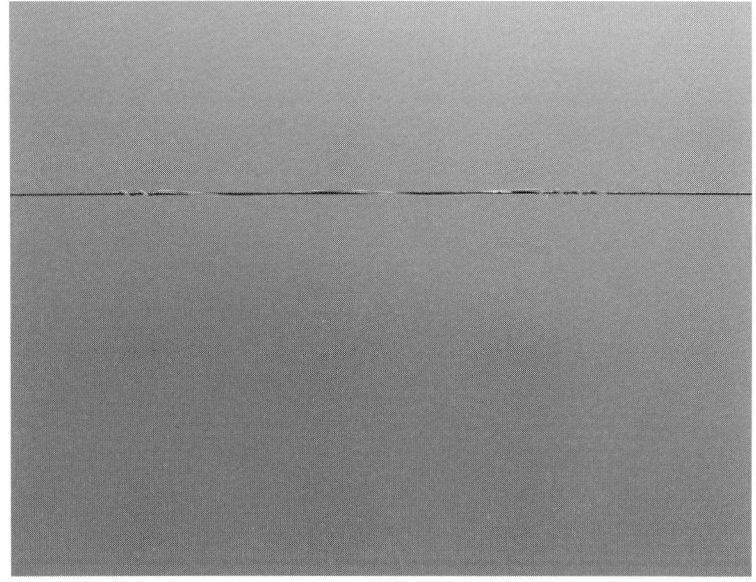

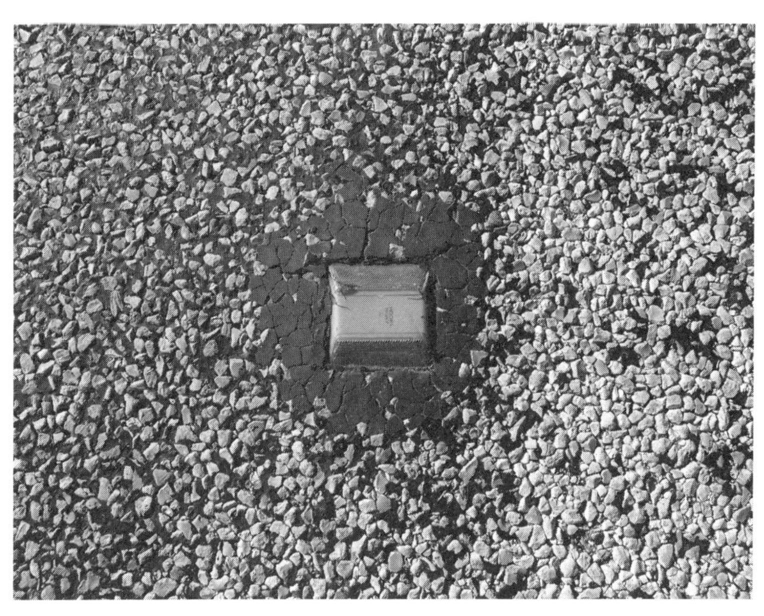

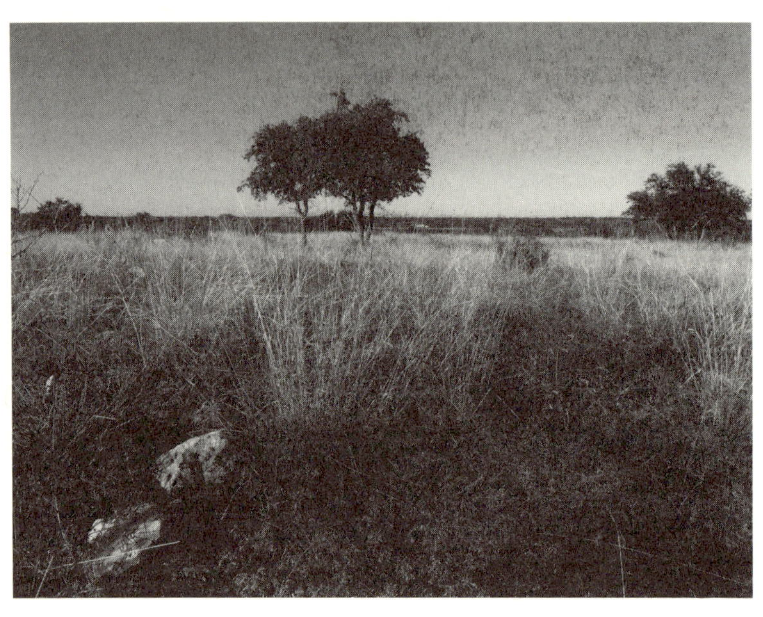

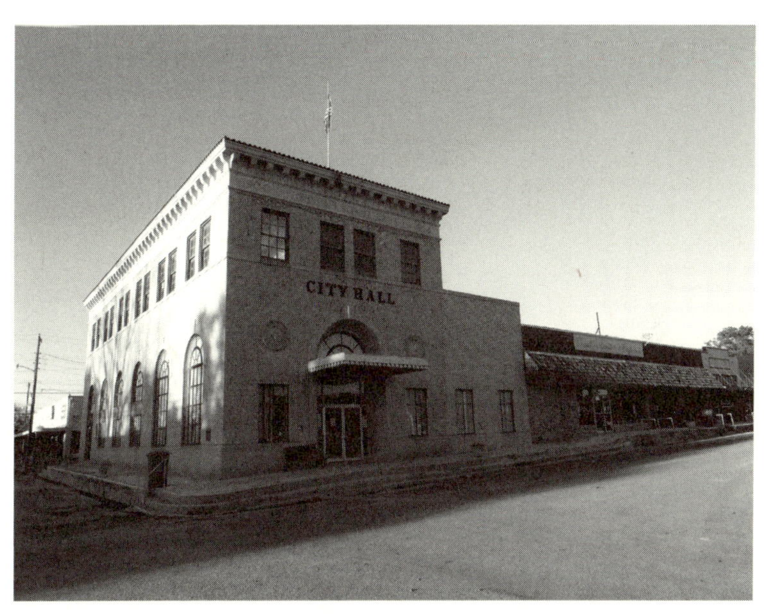
CITY HALL

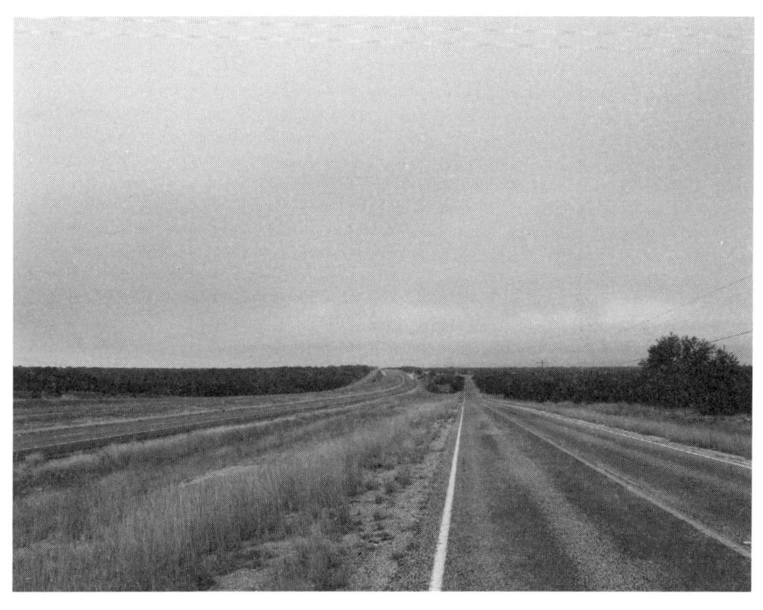

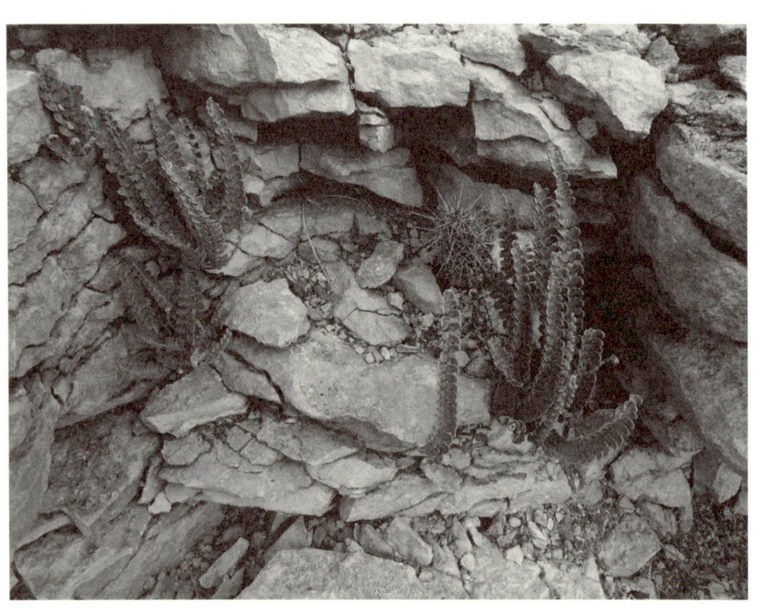

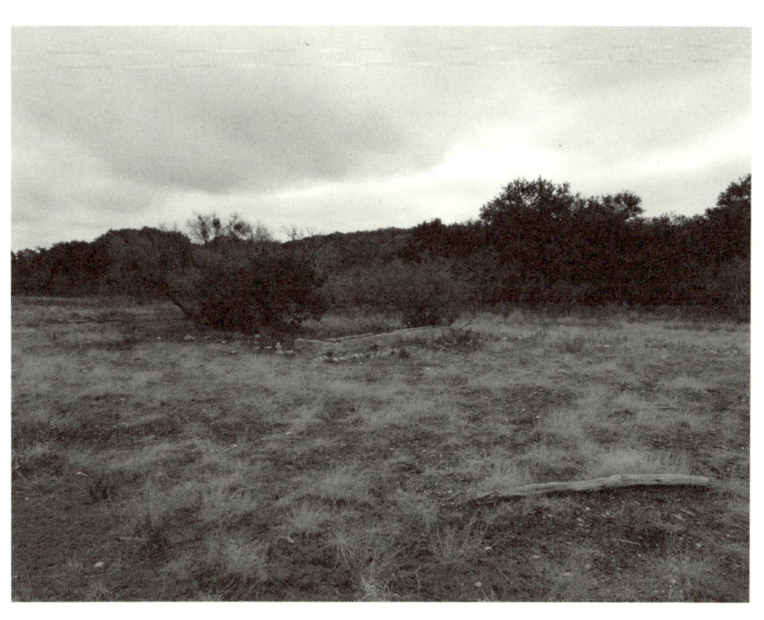

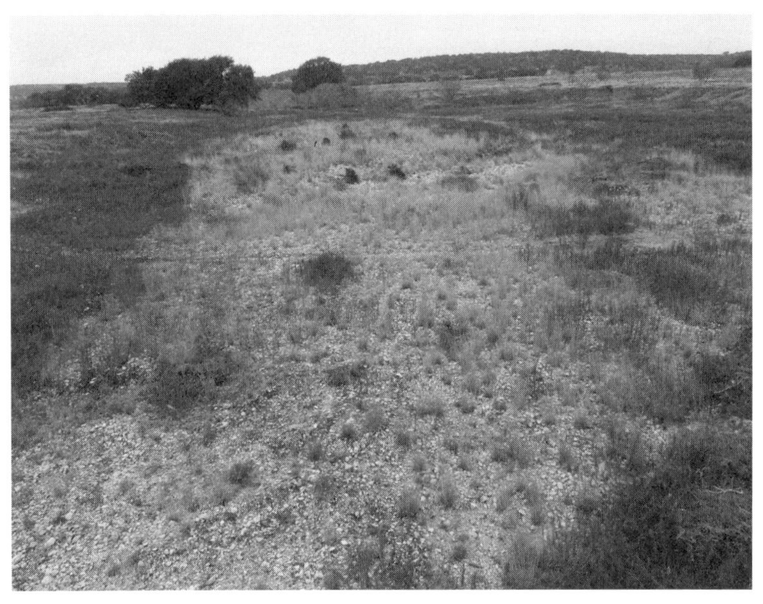

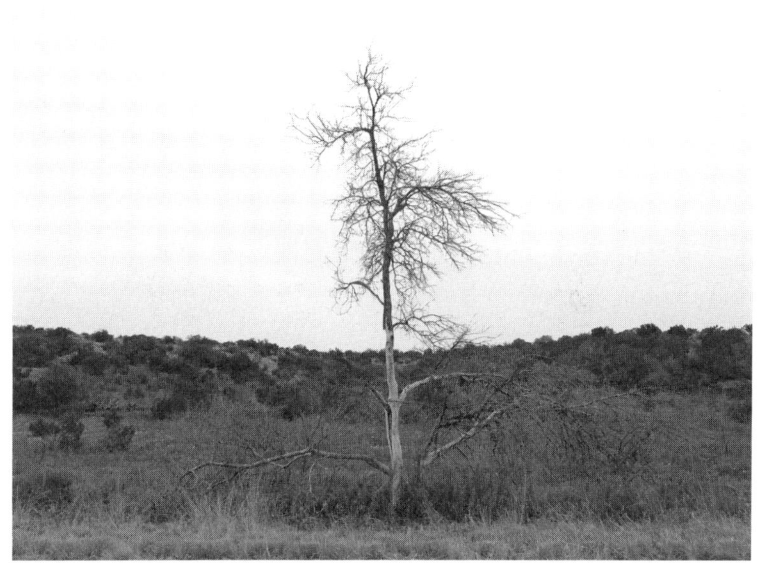

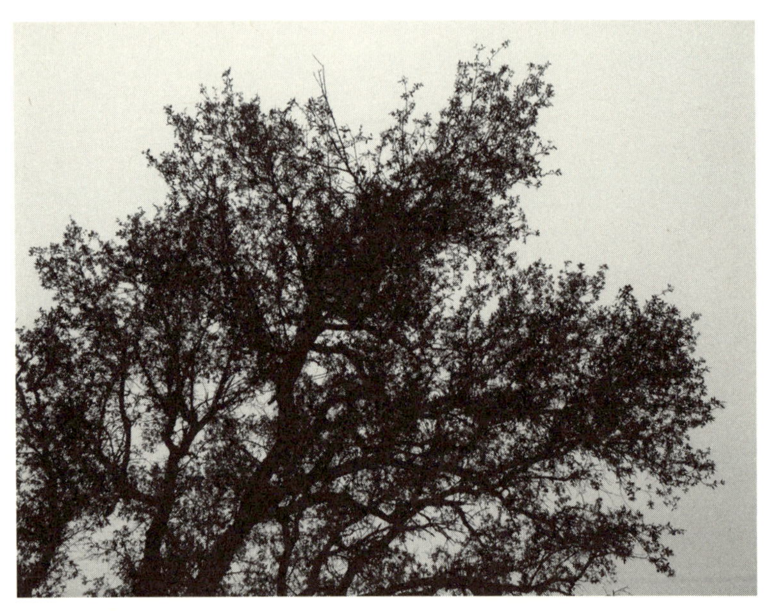

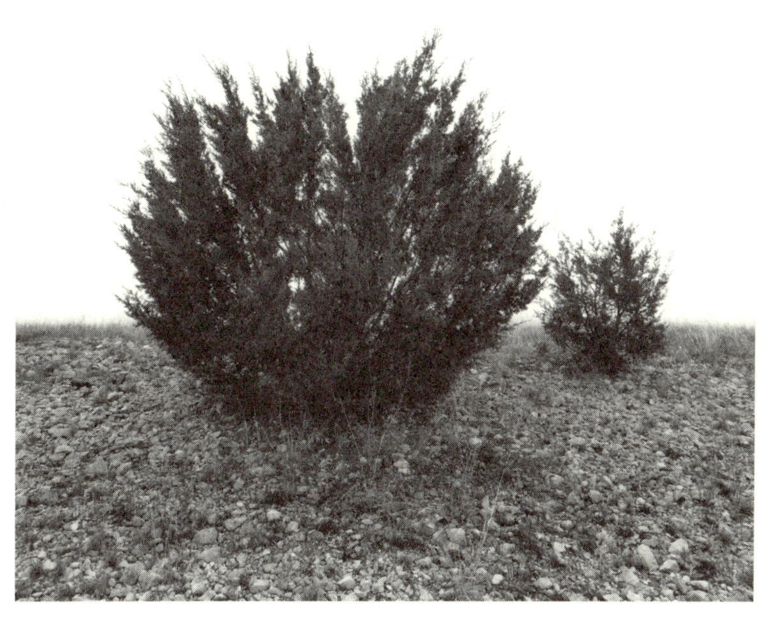

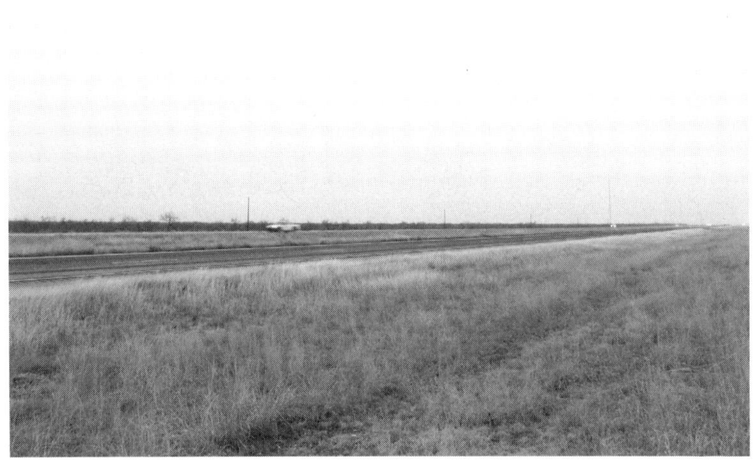

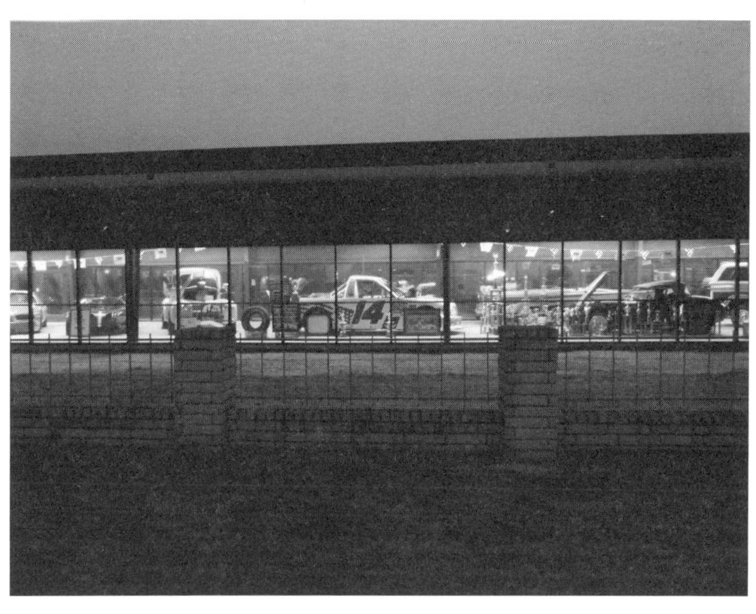

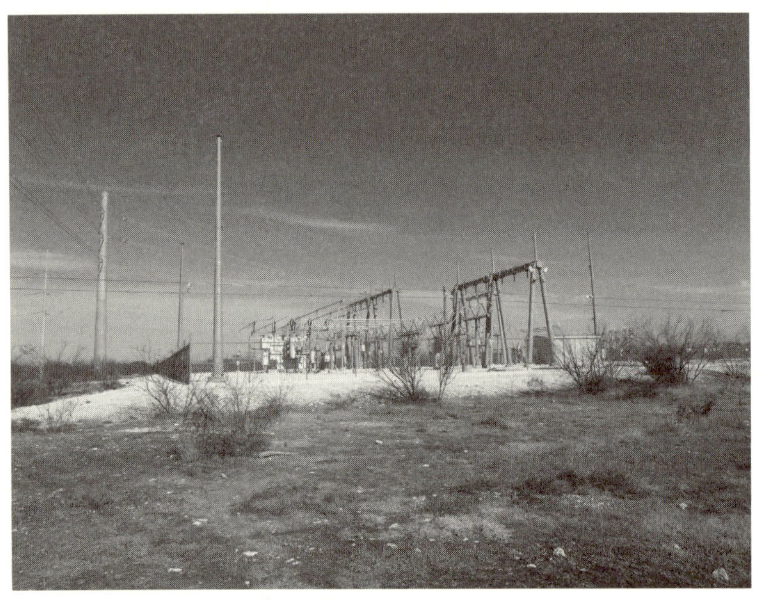

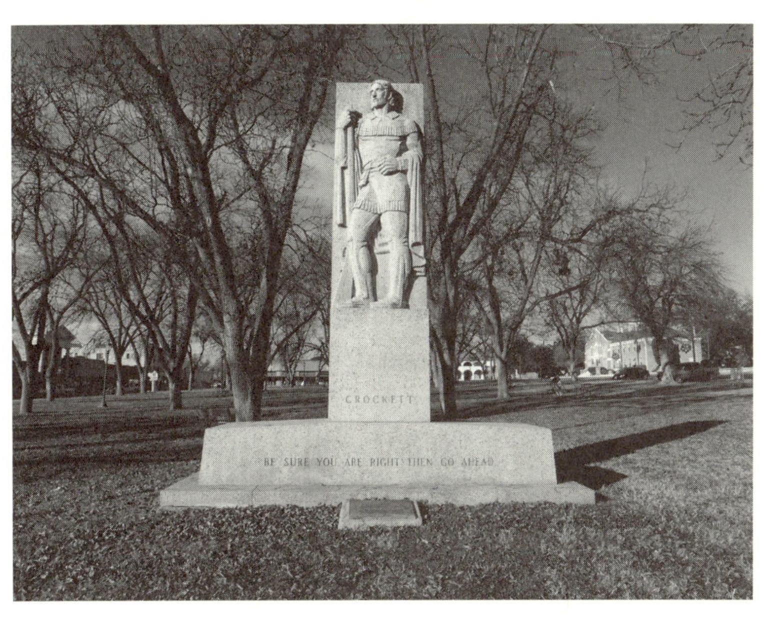
CROCKETT
BE SURE YOU ARE RIGHT THEN GO AHEAD

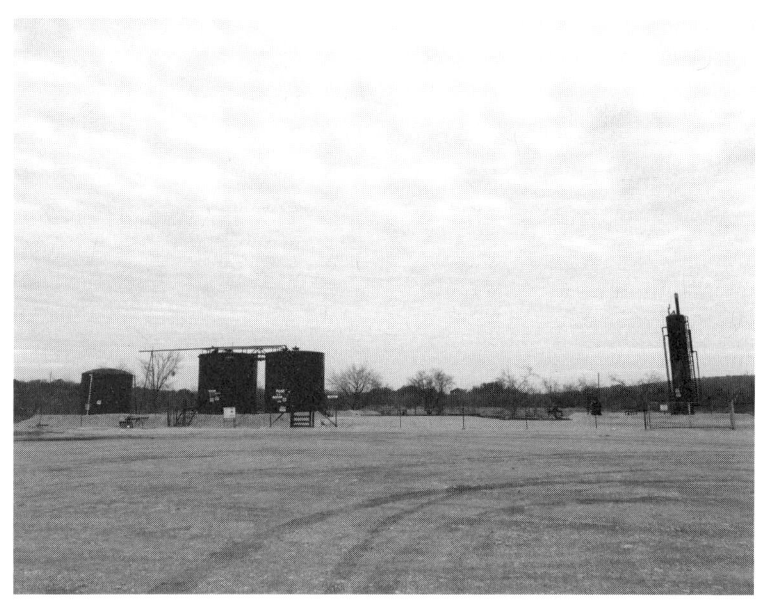

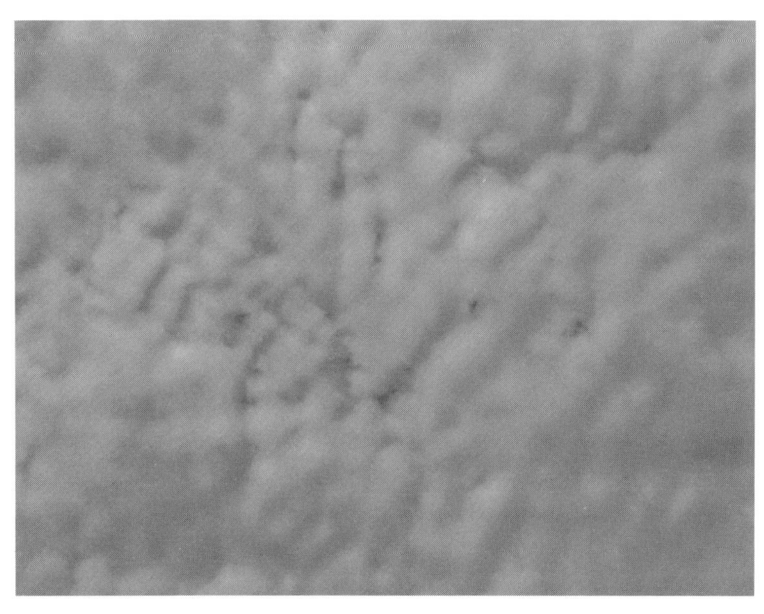

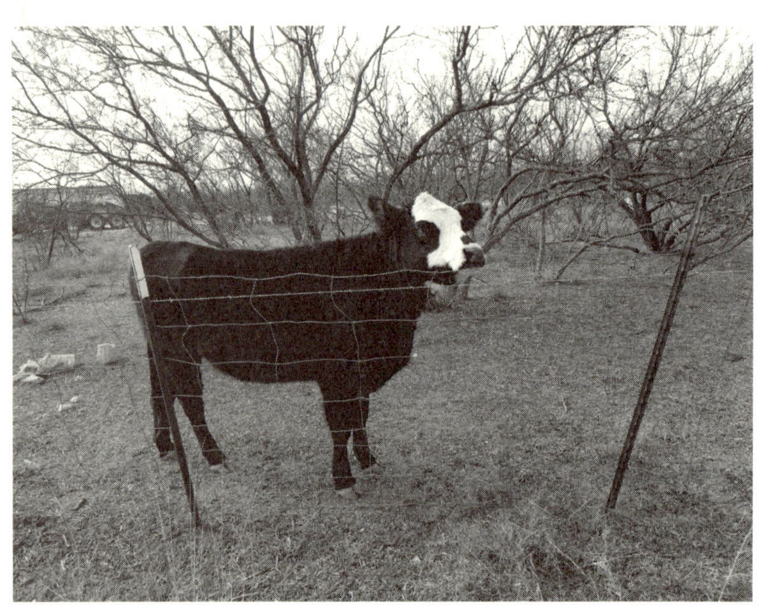

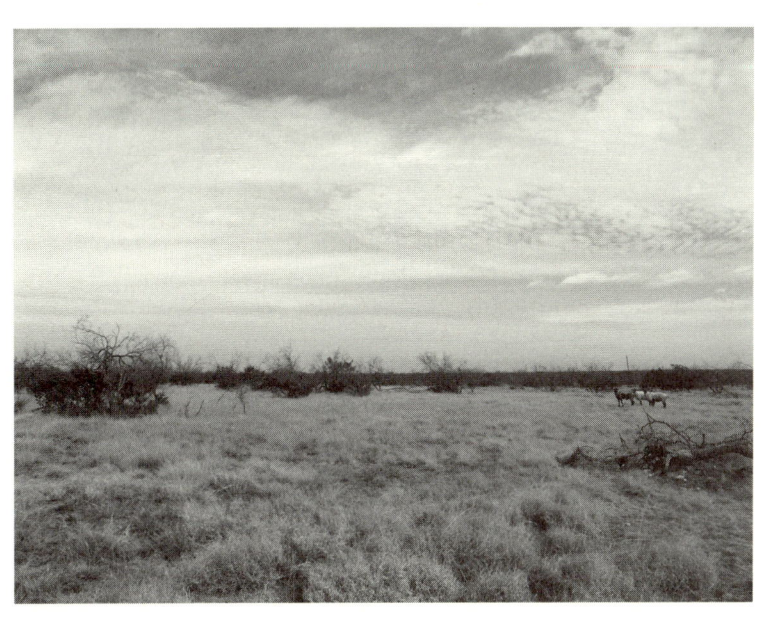

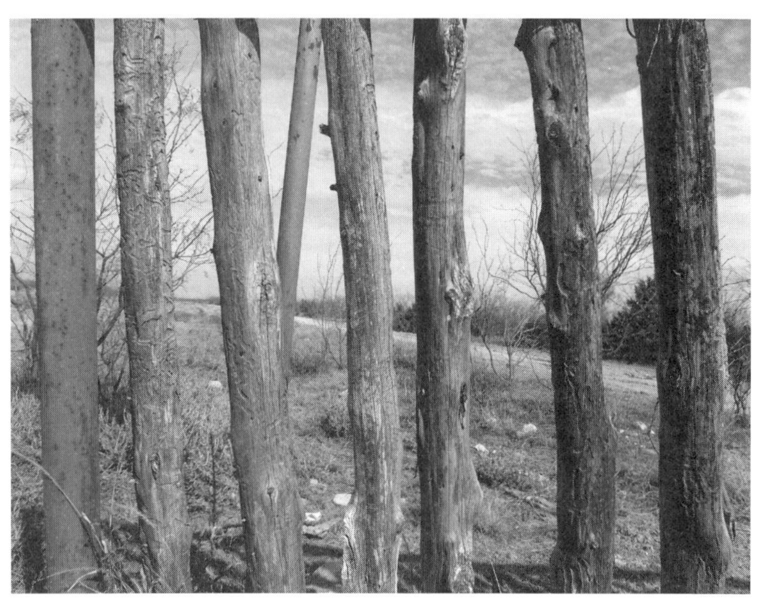

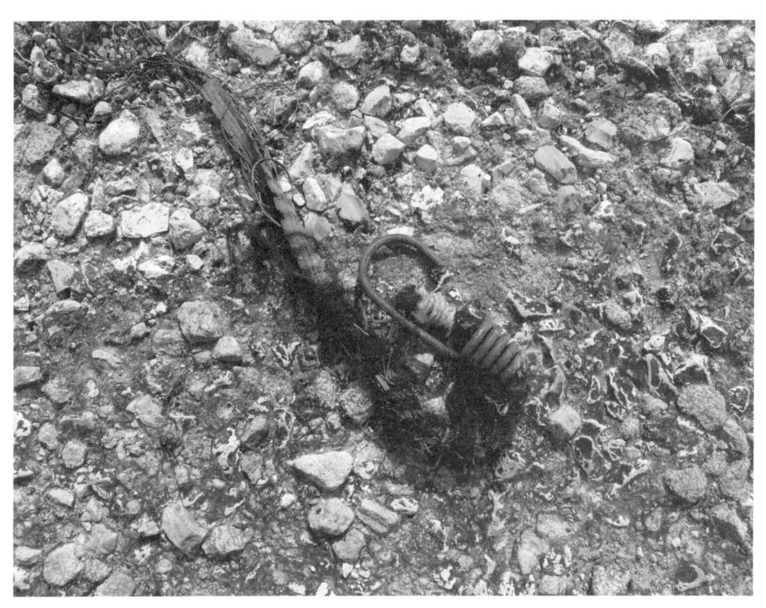

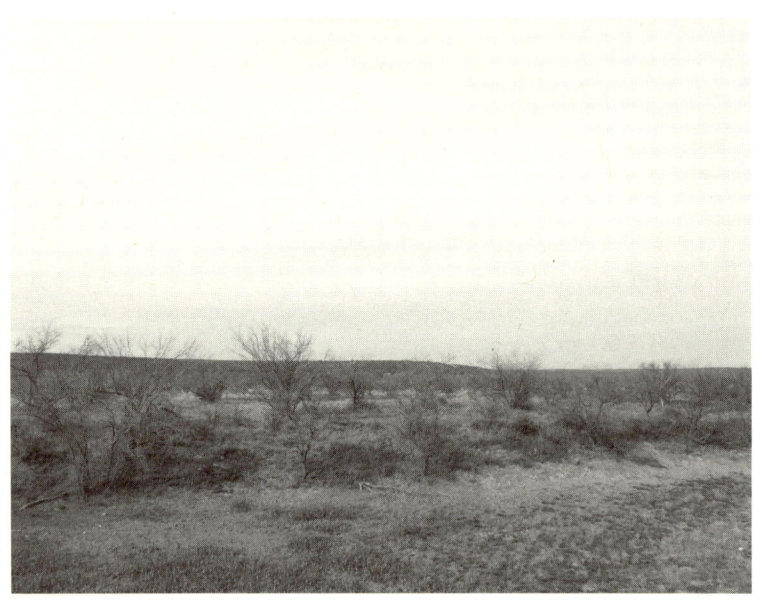

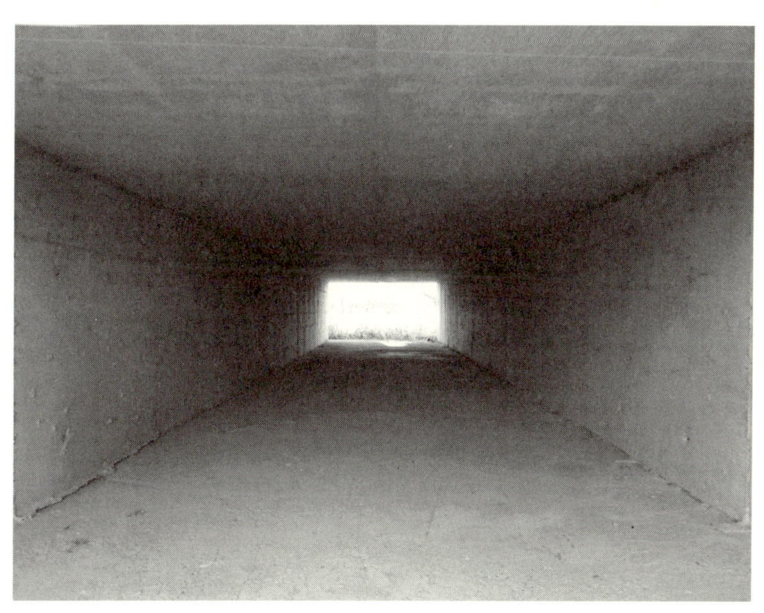

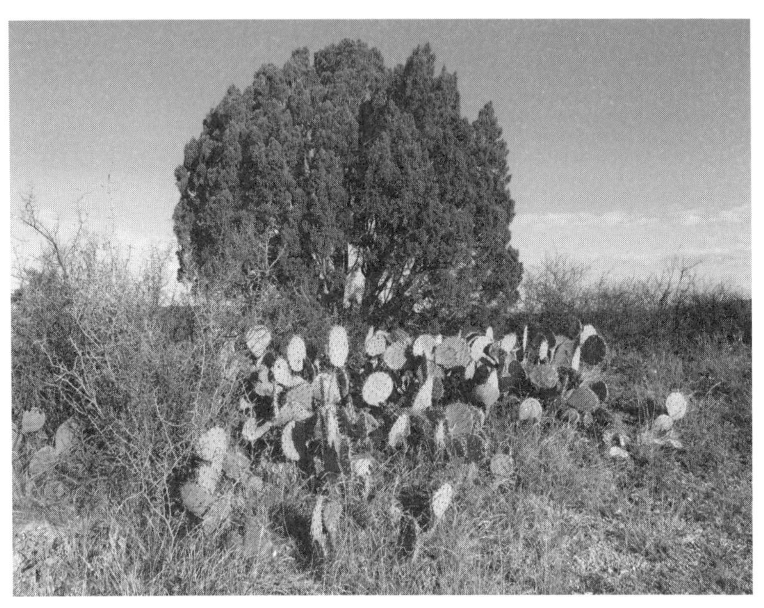

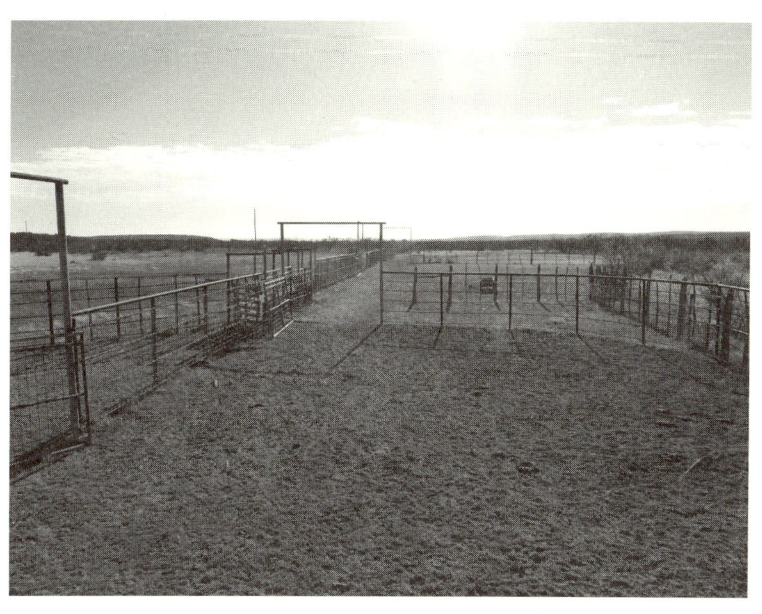

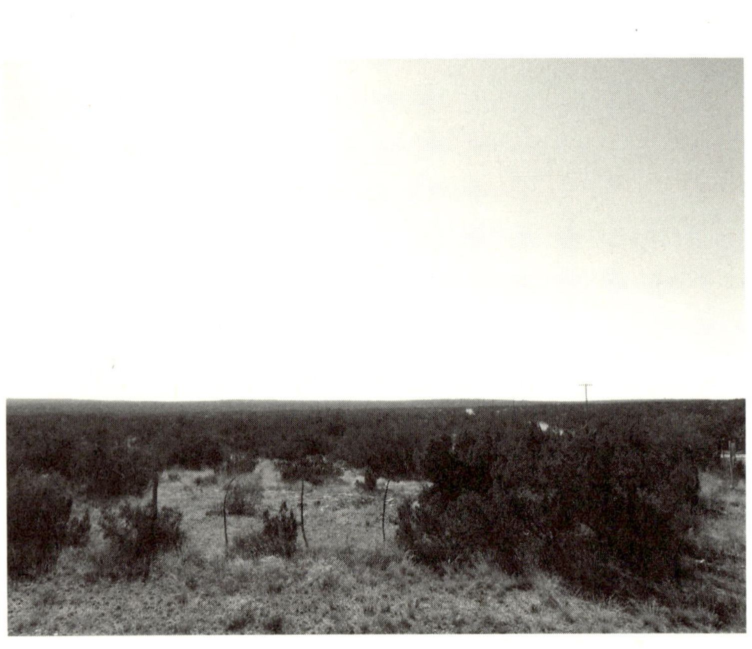

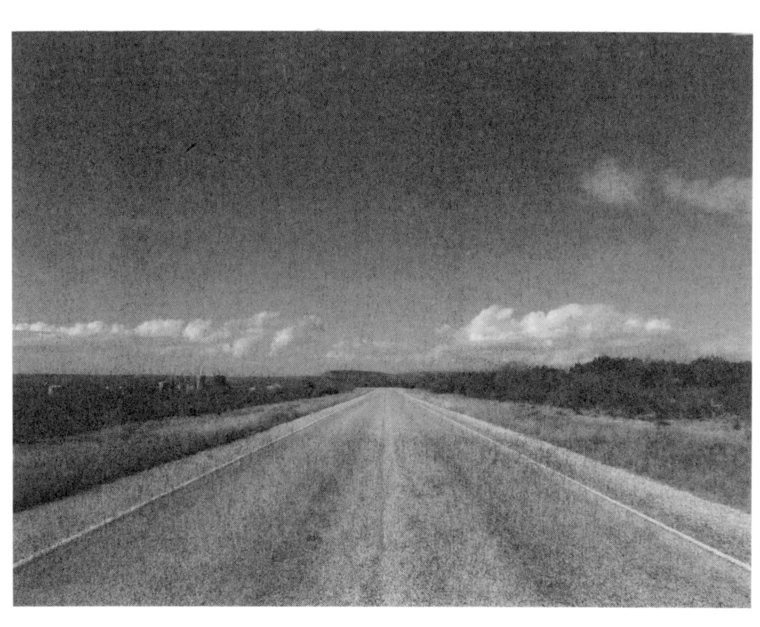

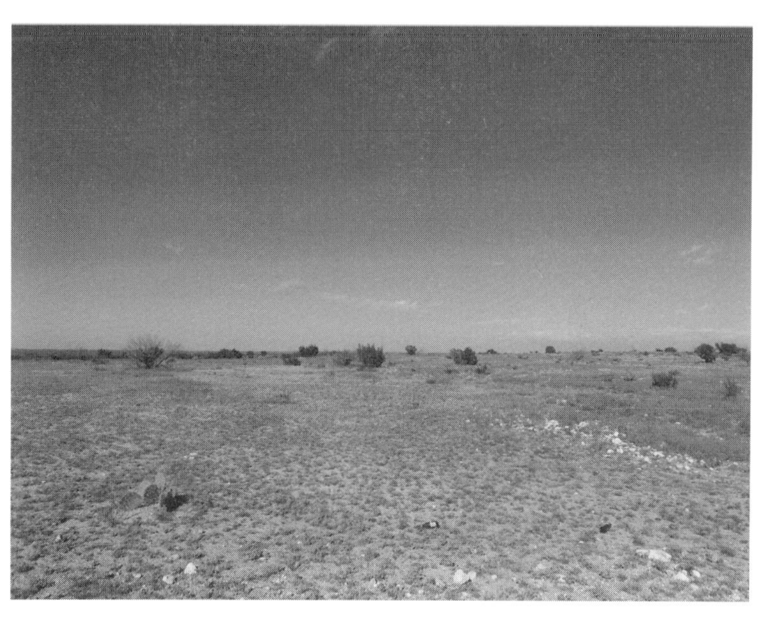

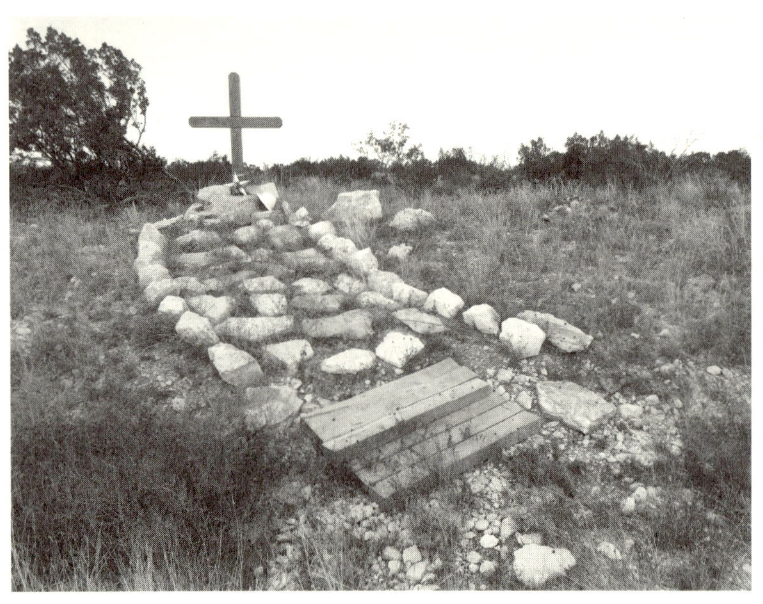

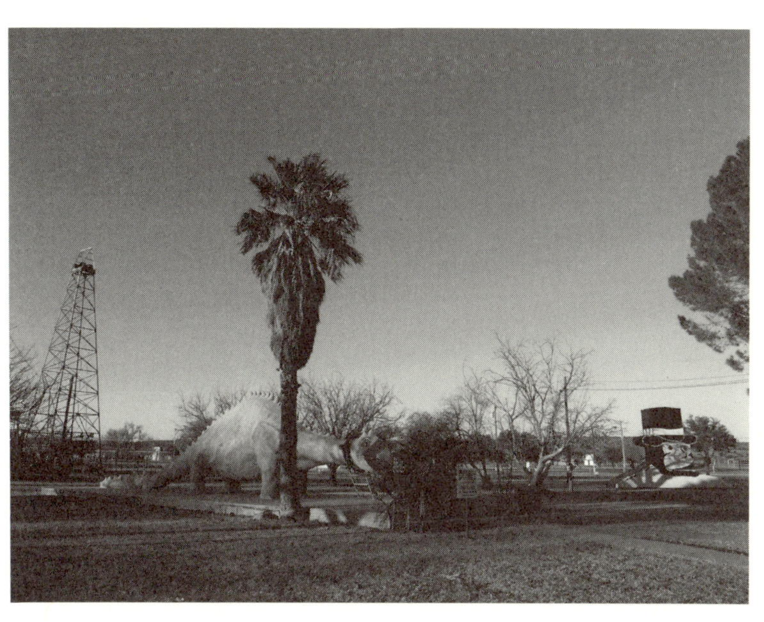

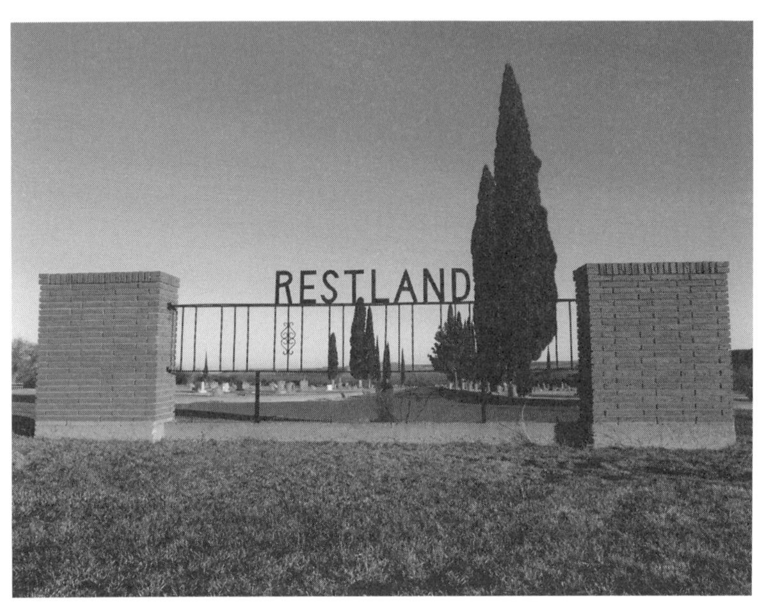
RESTLAND

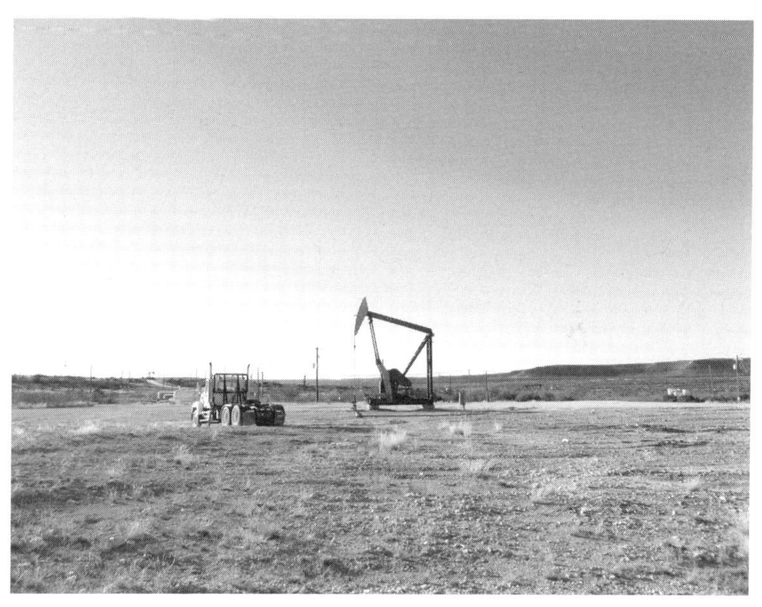

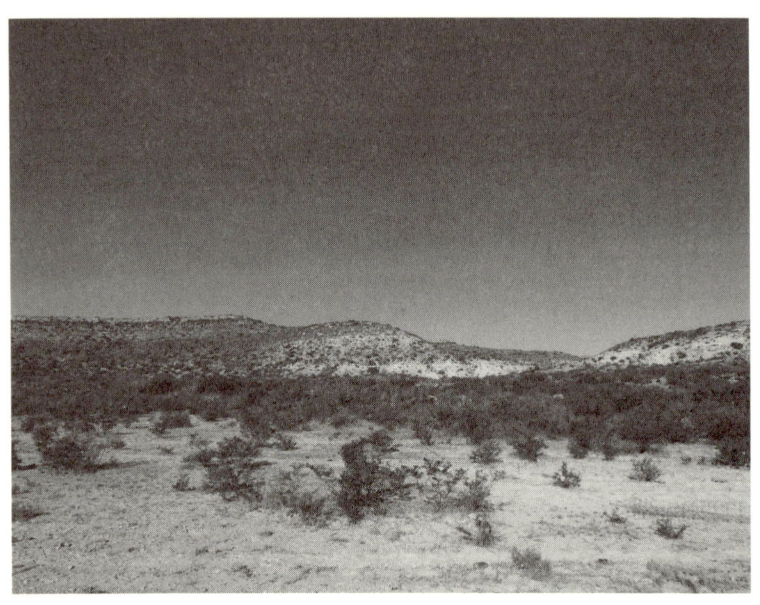

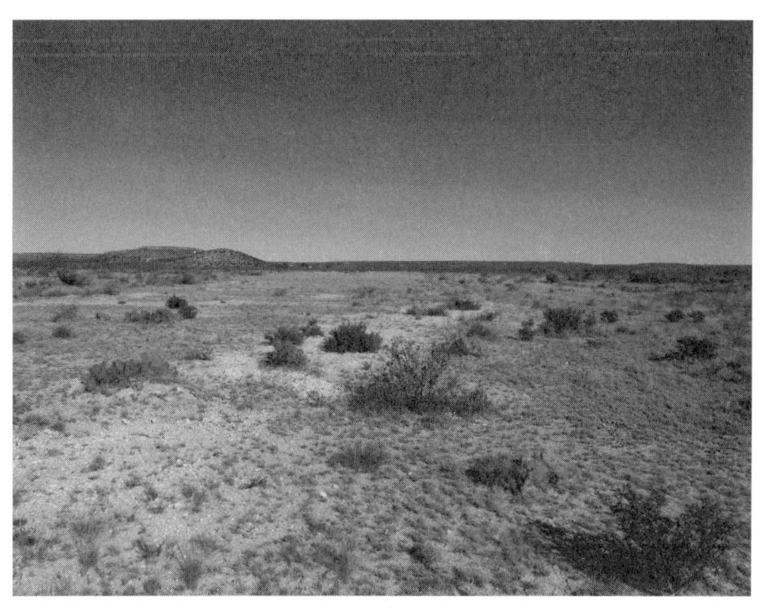

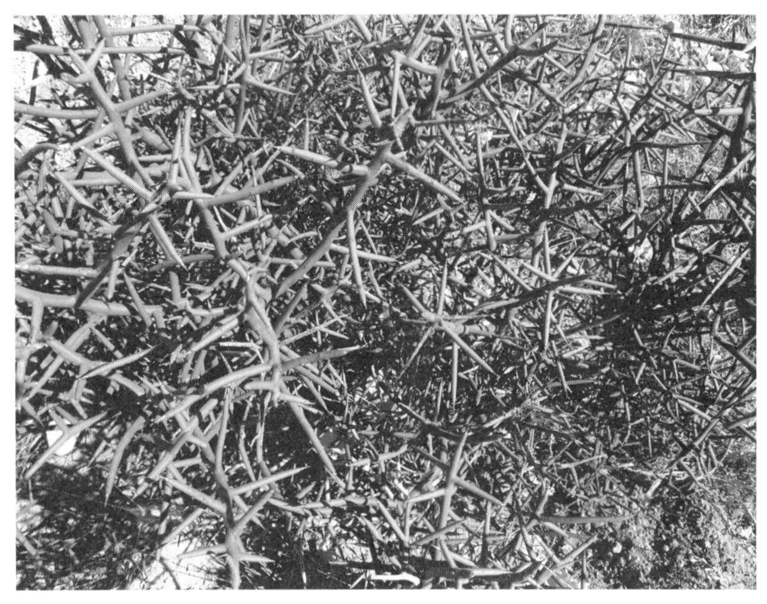

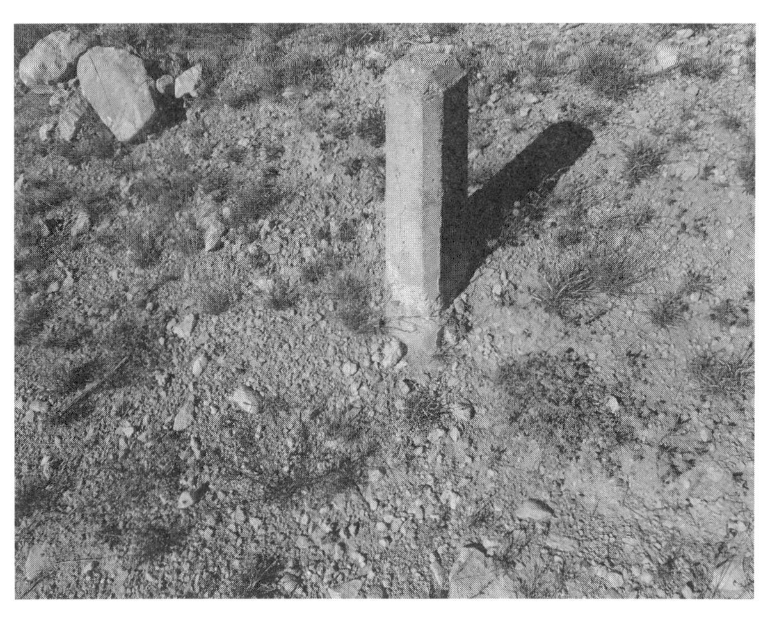

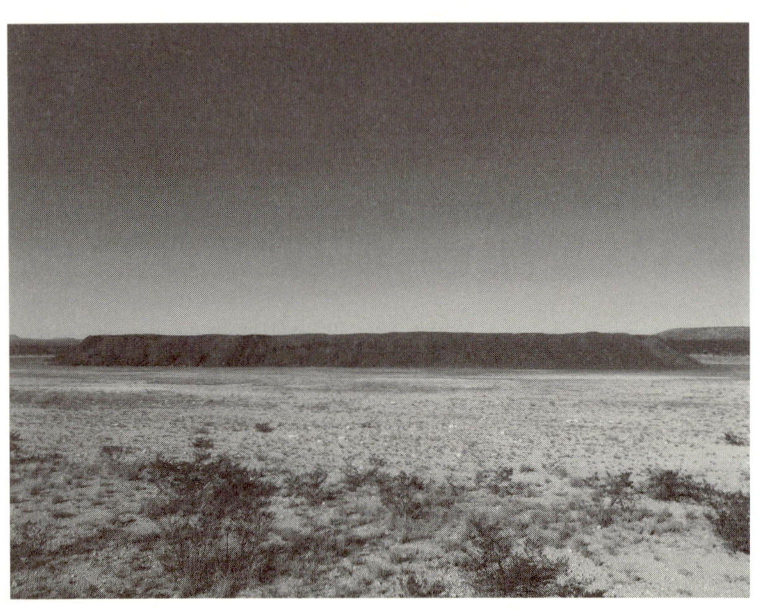

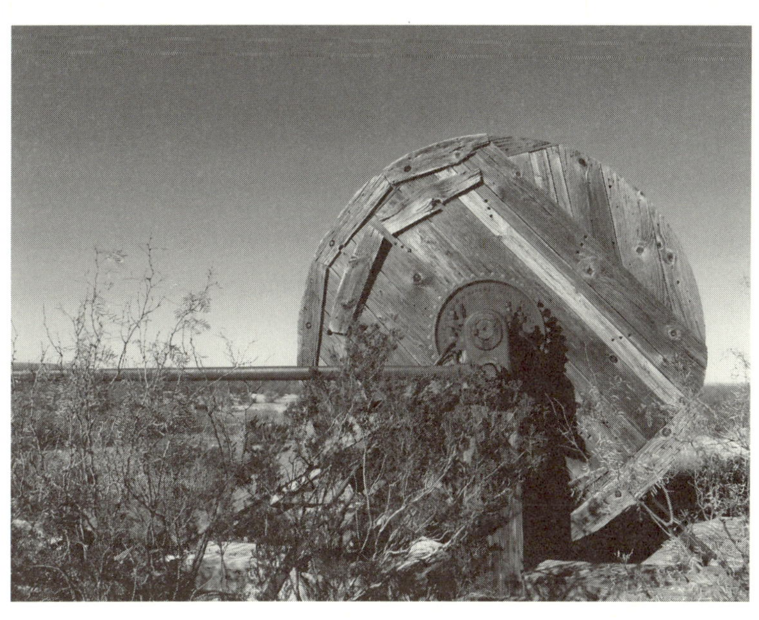

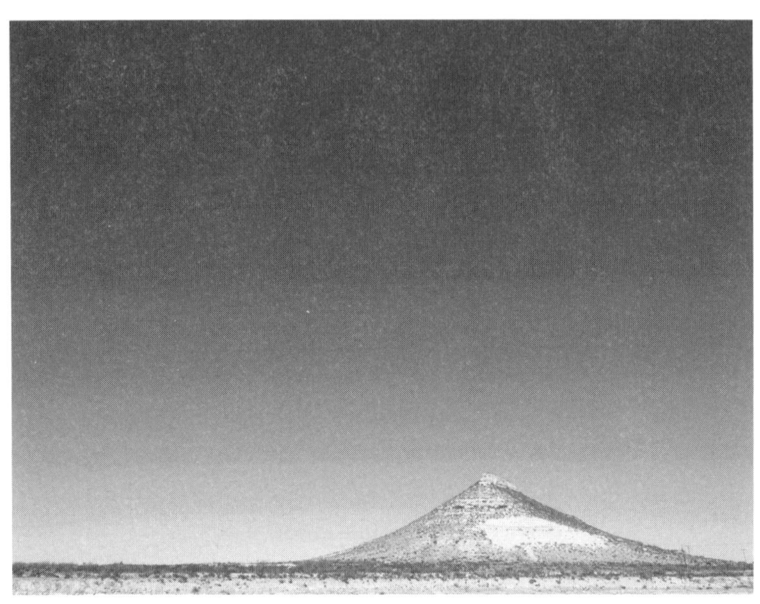

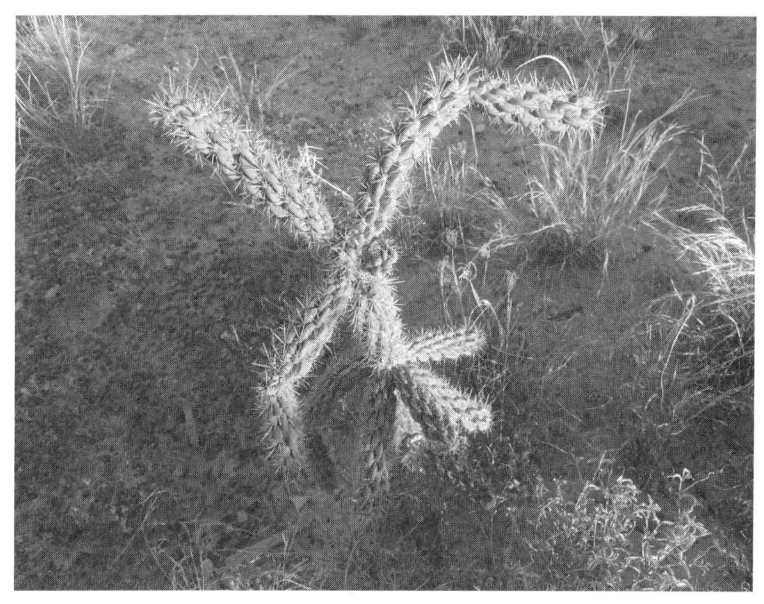

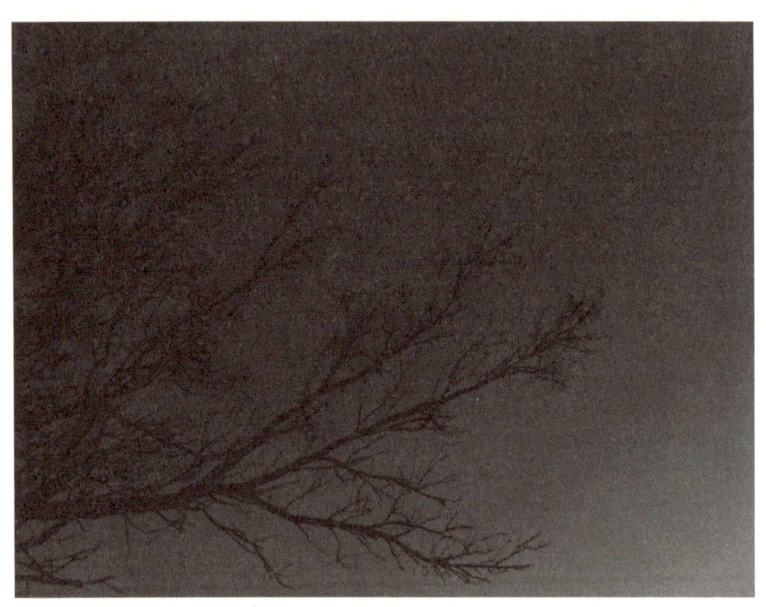

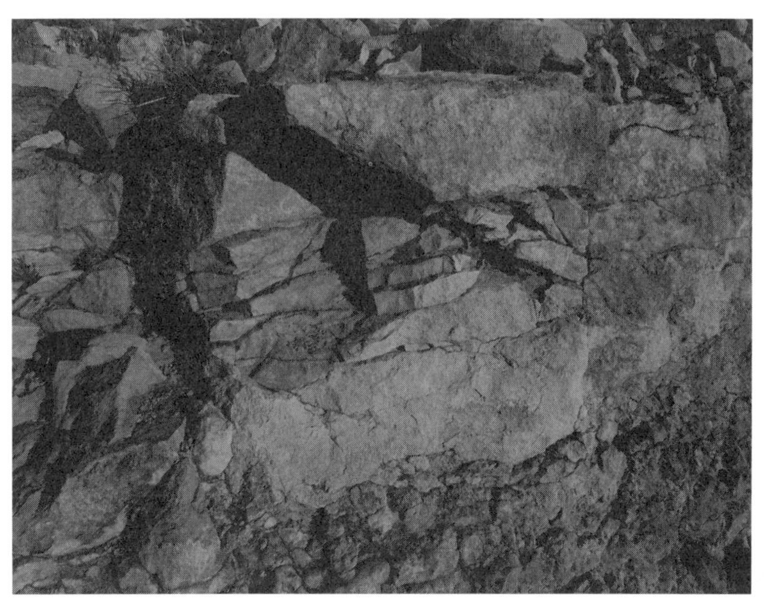

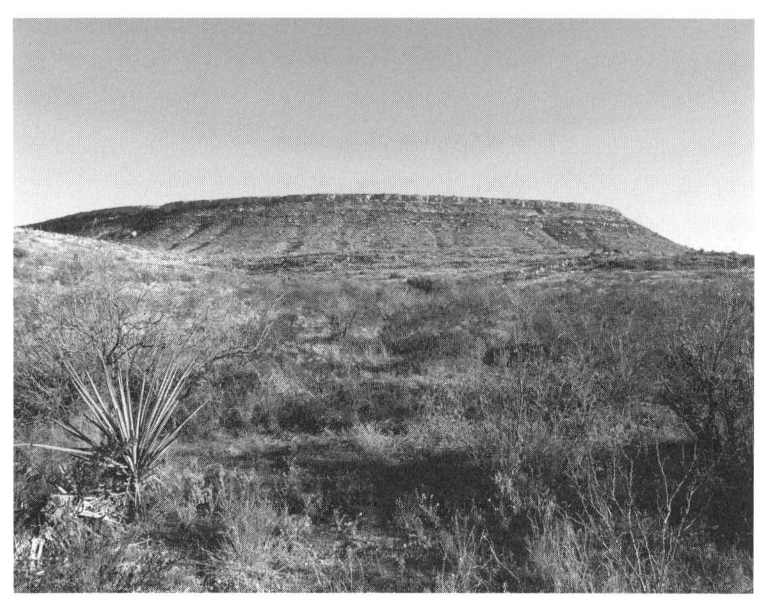

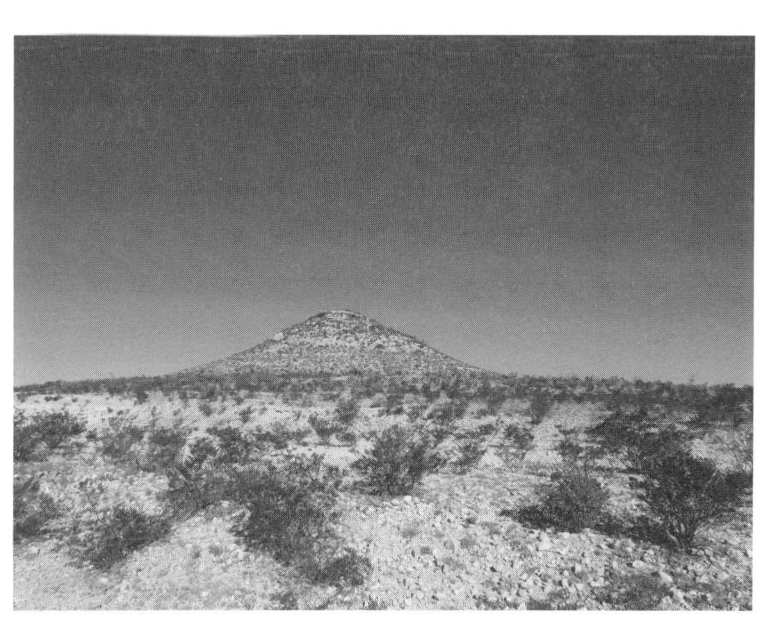

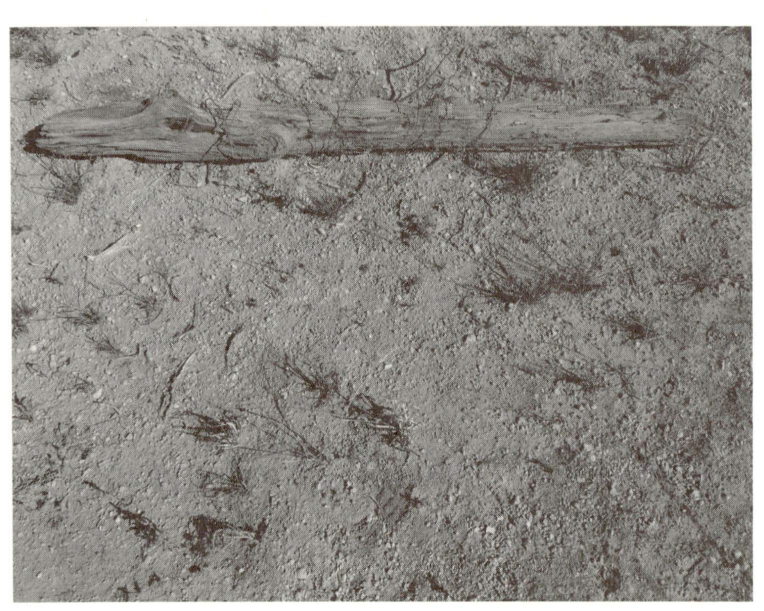

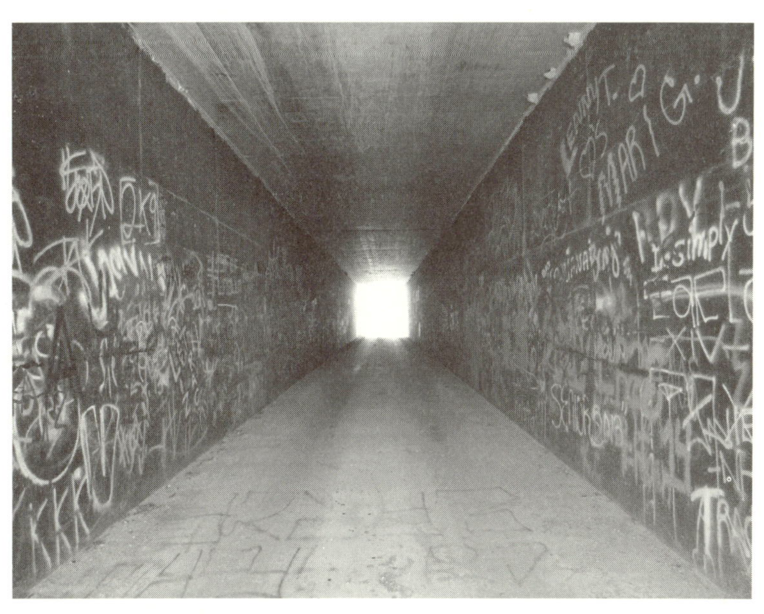

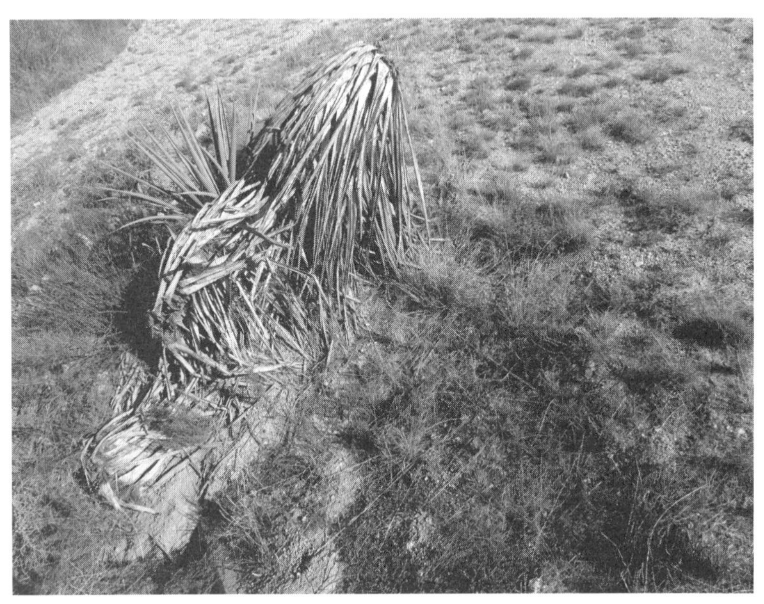

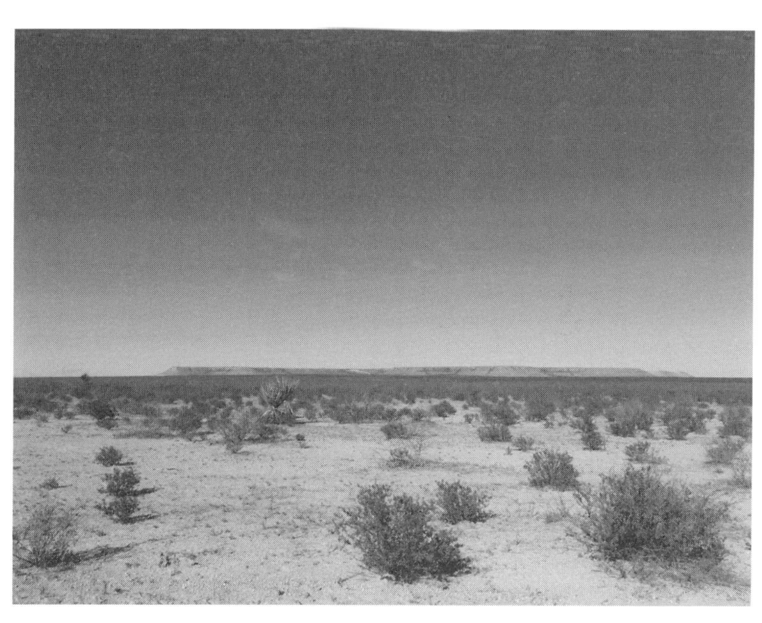

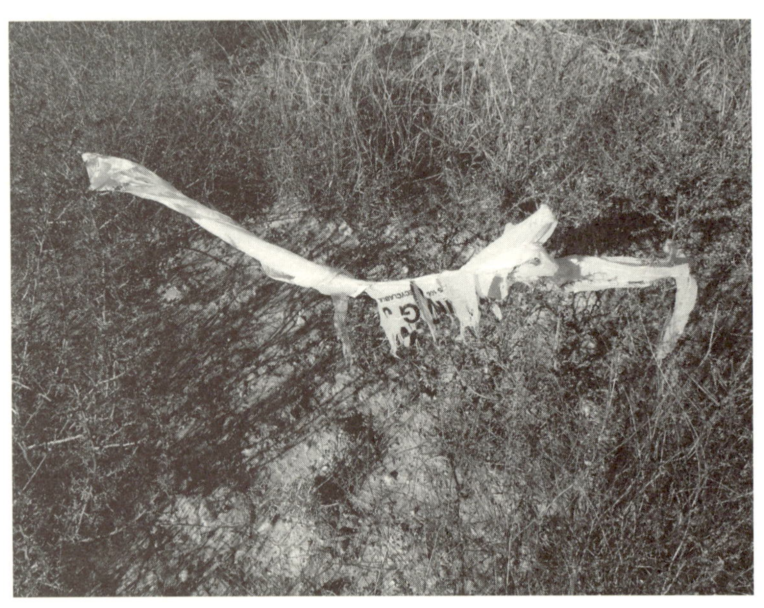

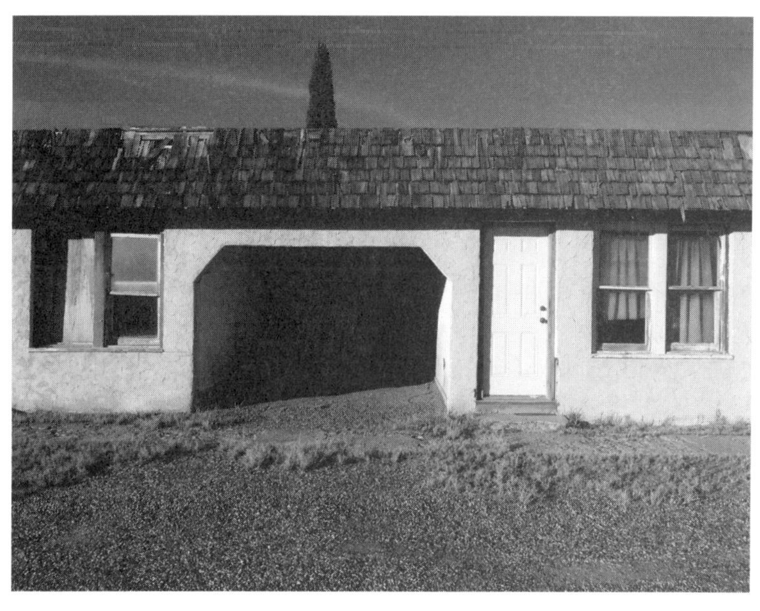

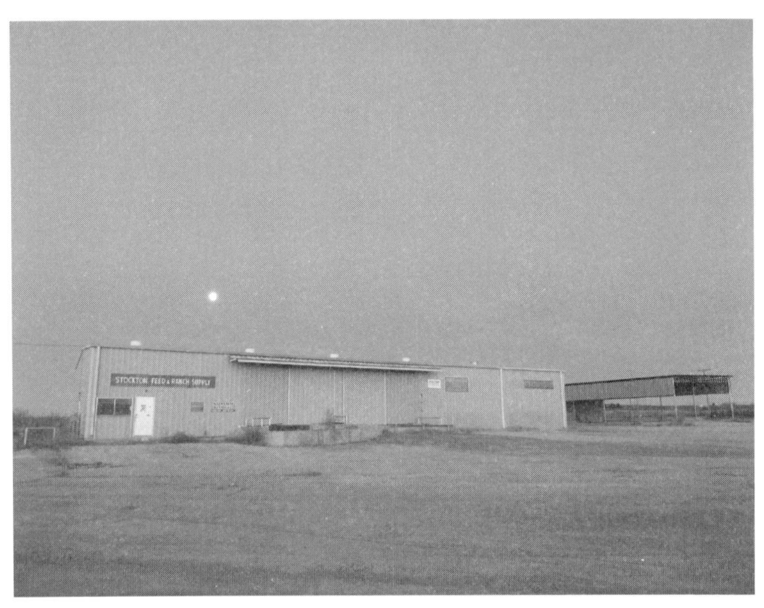
STOCKTON FEED & RANCH SUPPLY

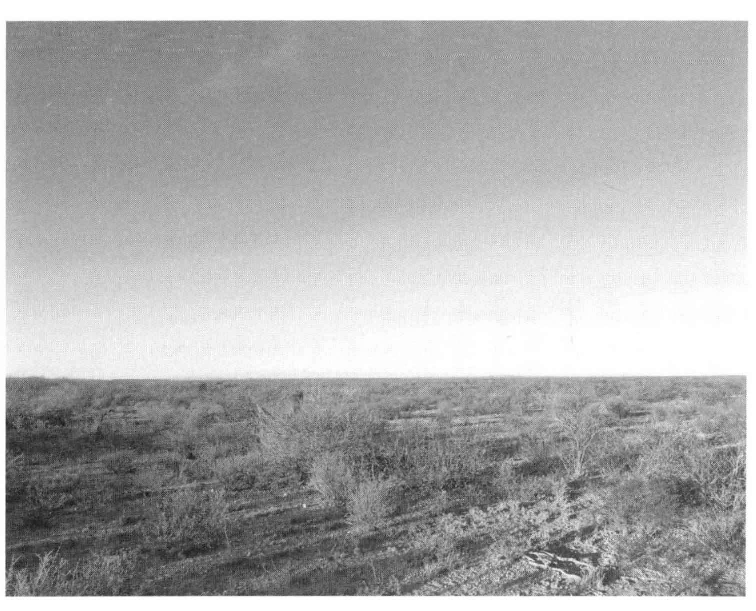

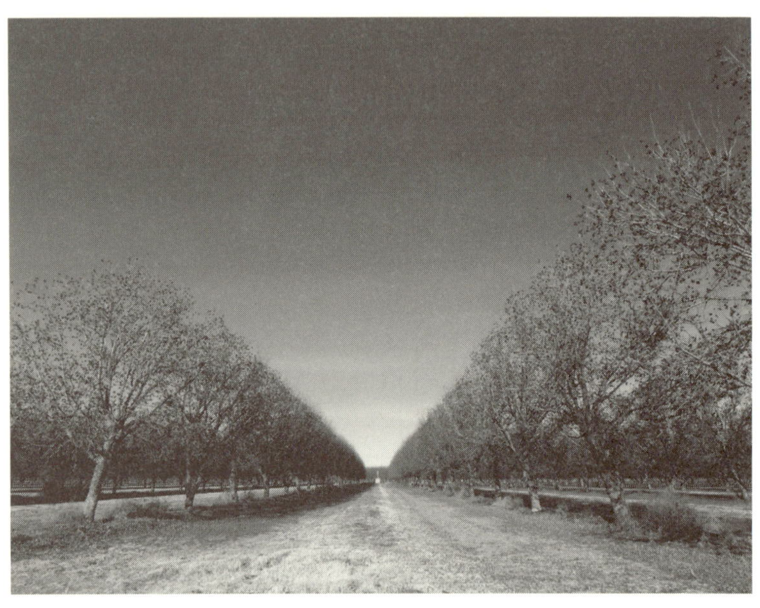

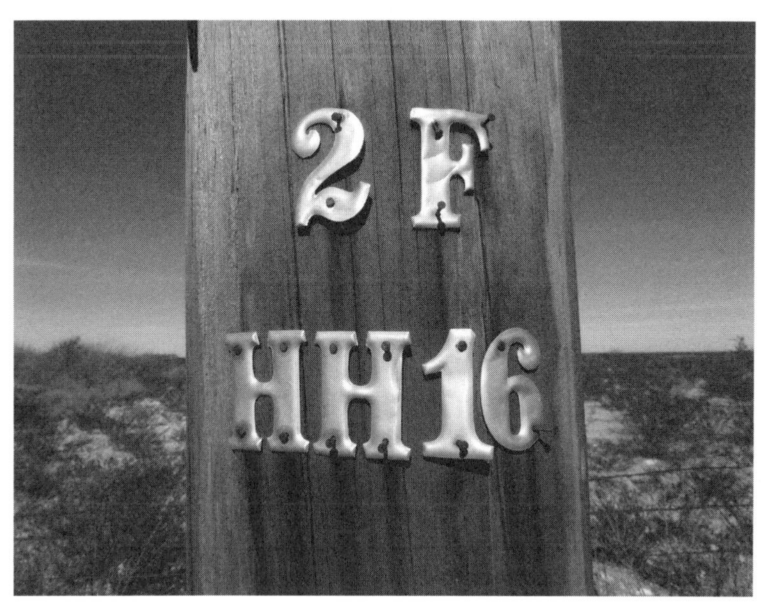
2 F
HH16

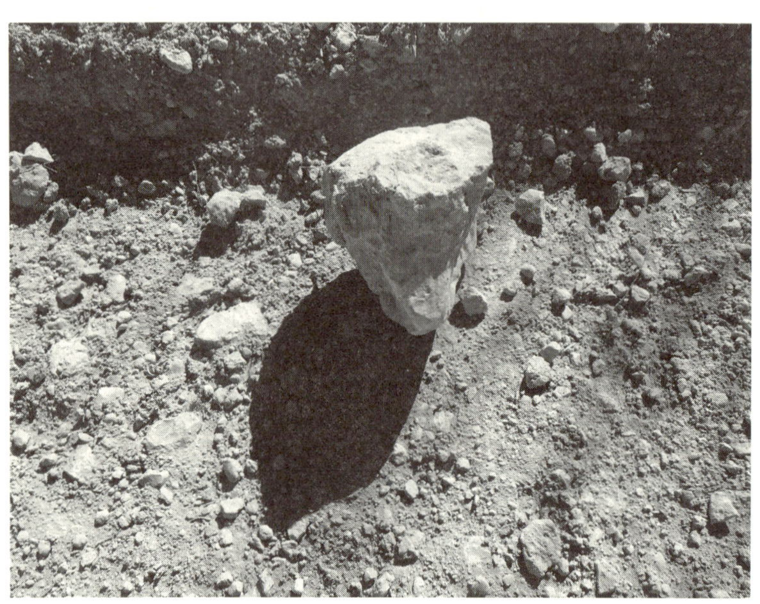

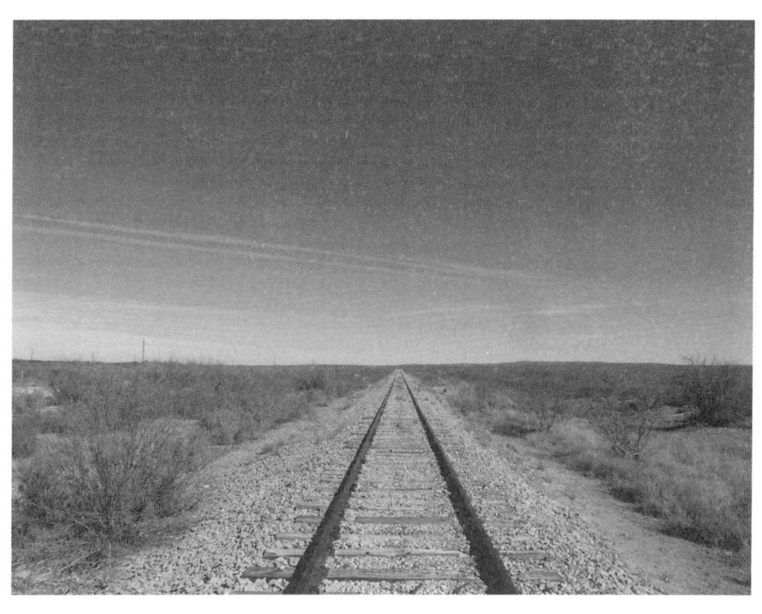

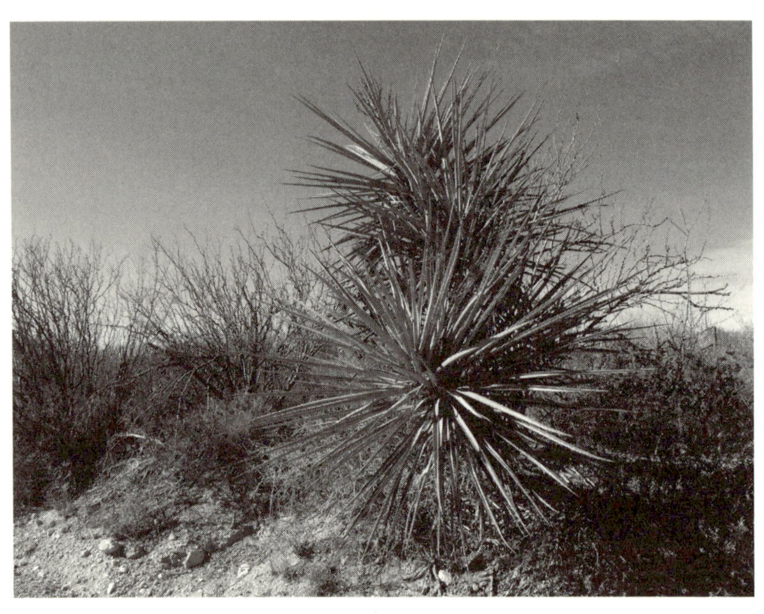

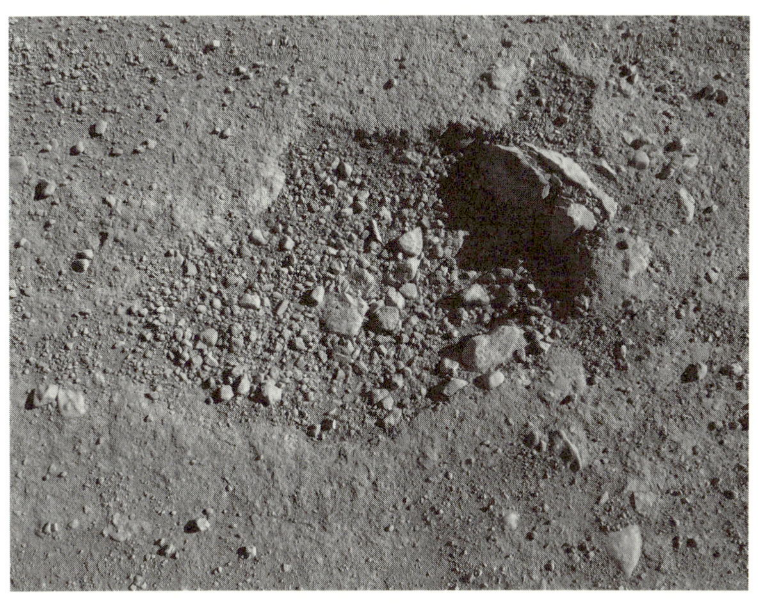

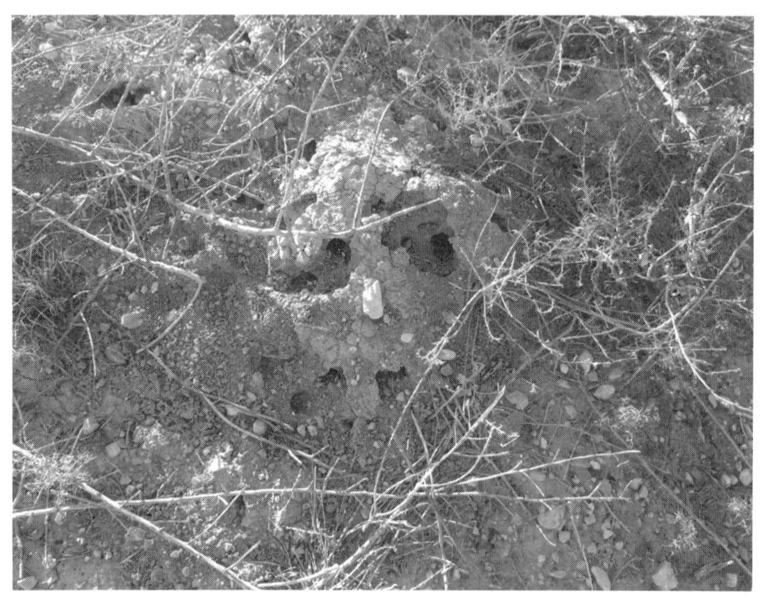

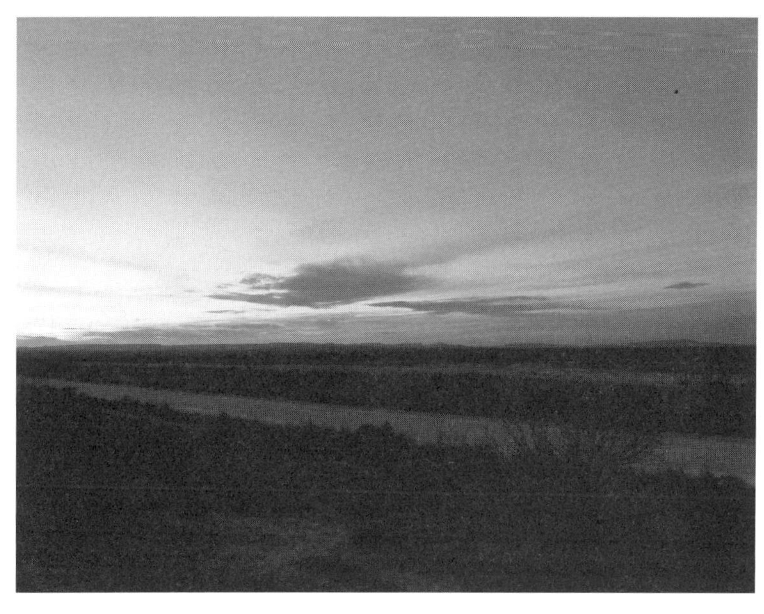

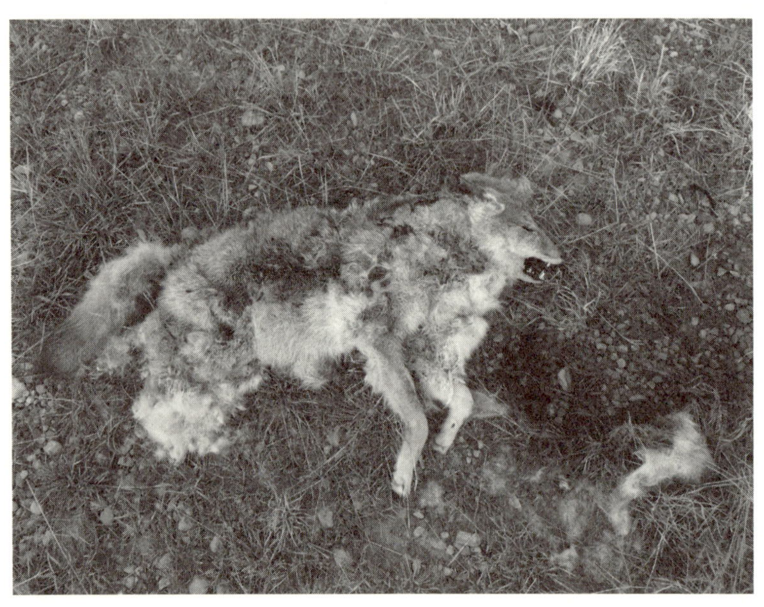

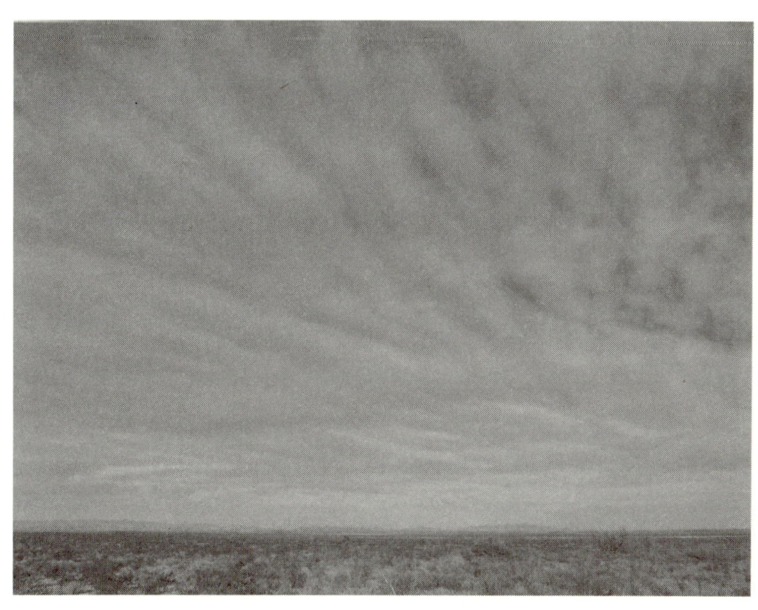

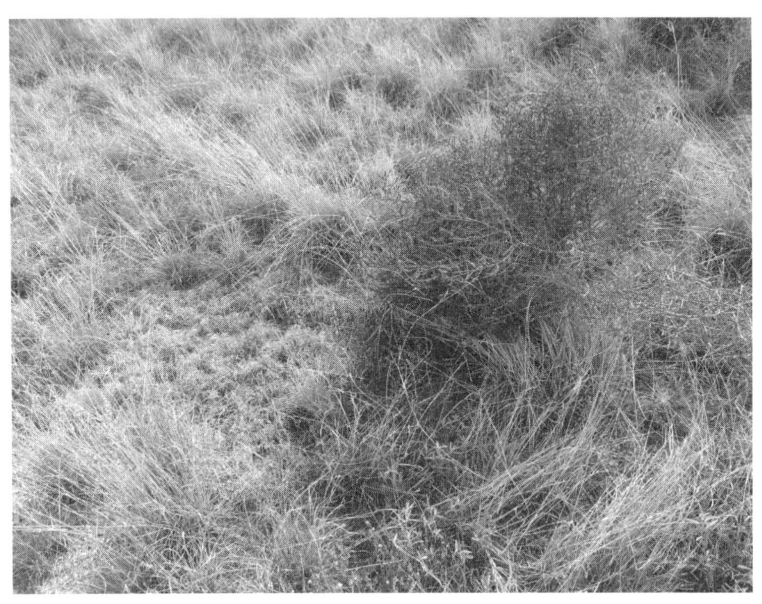

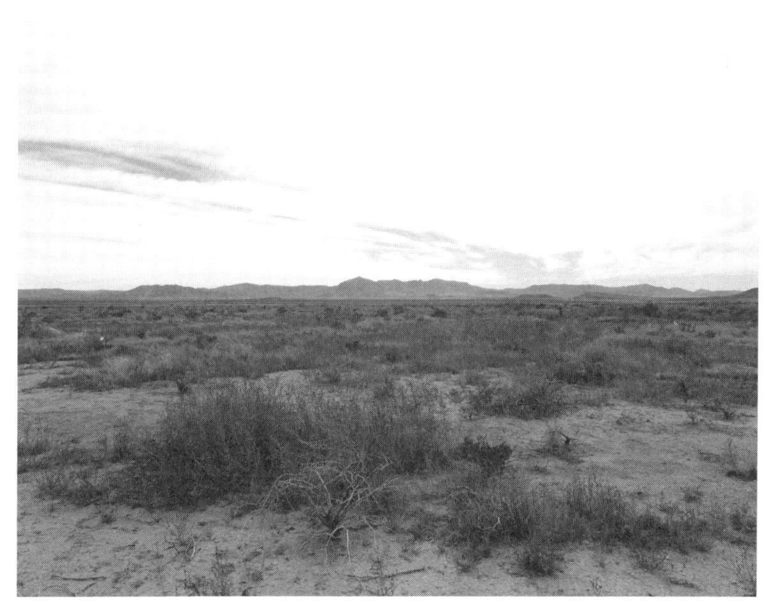

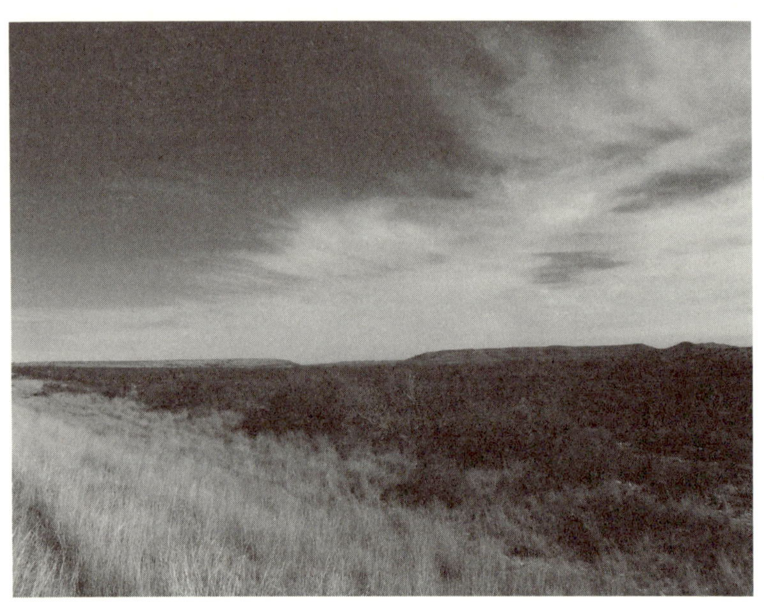

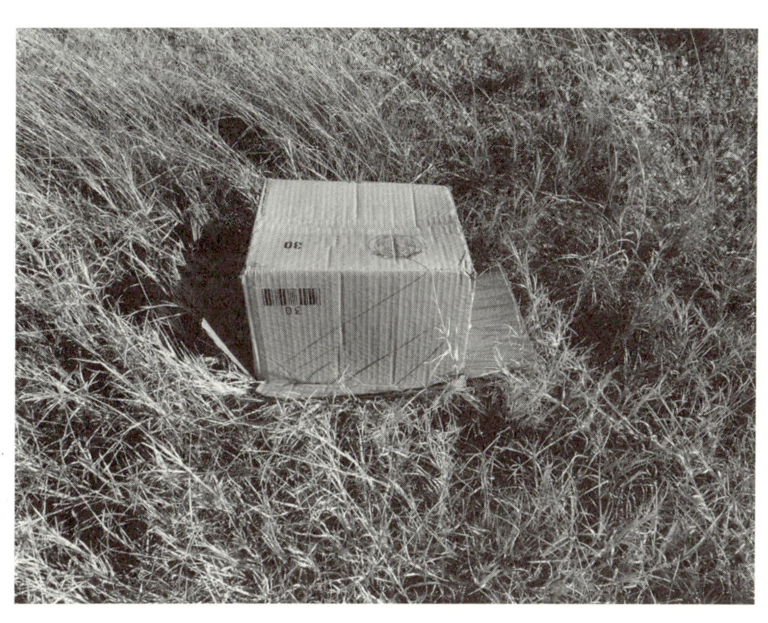

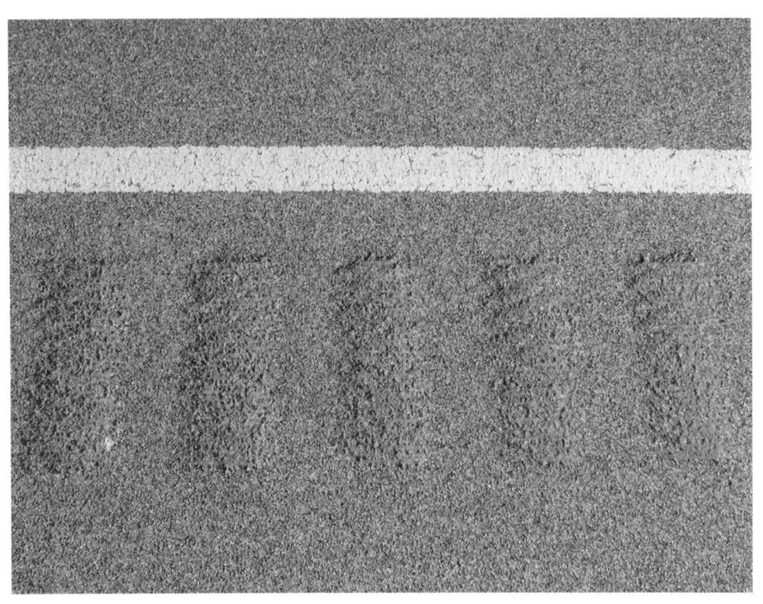

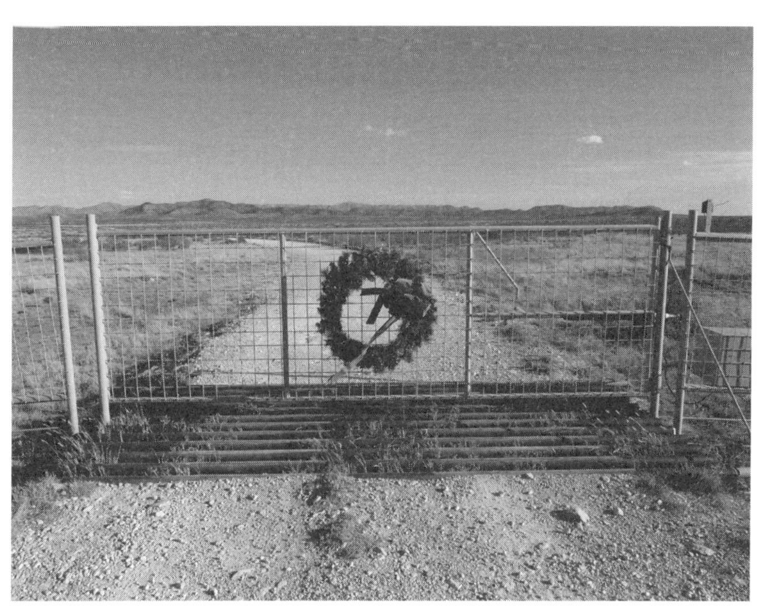

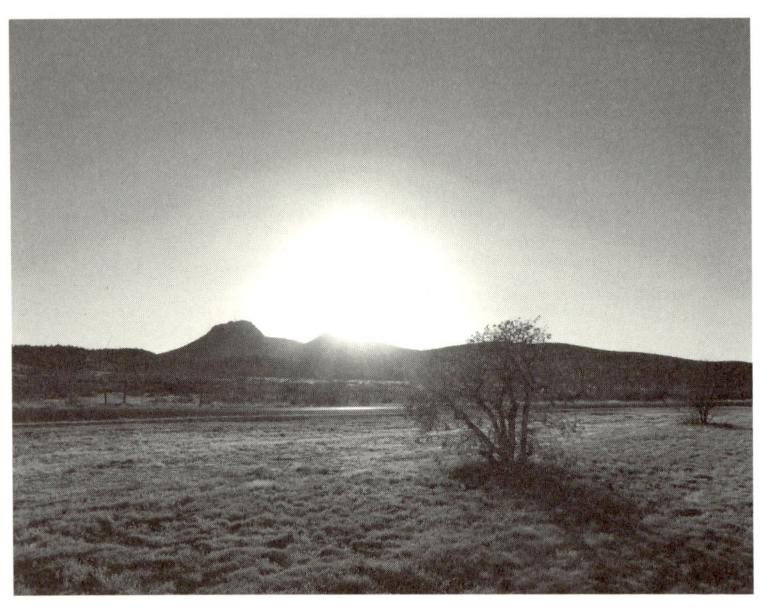

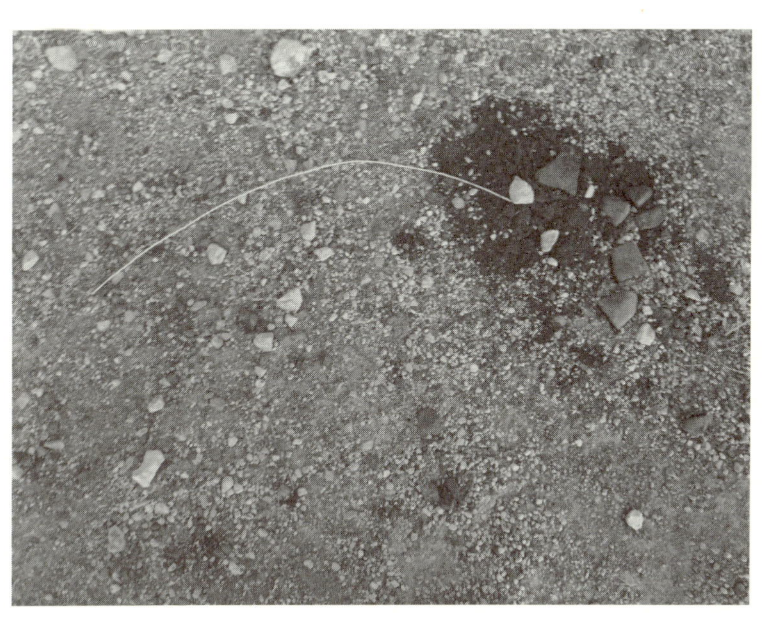

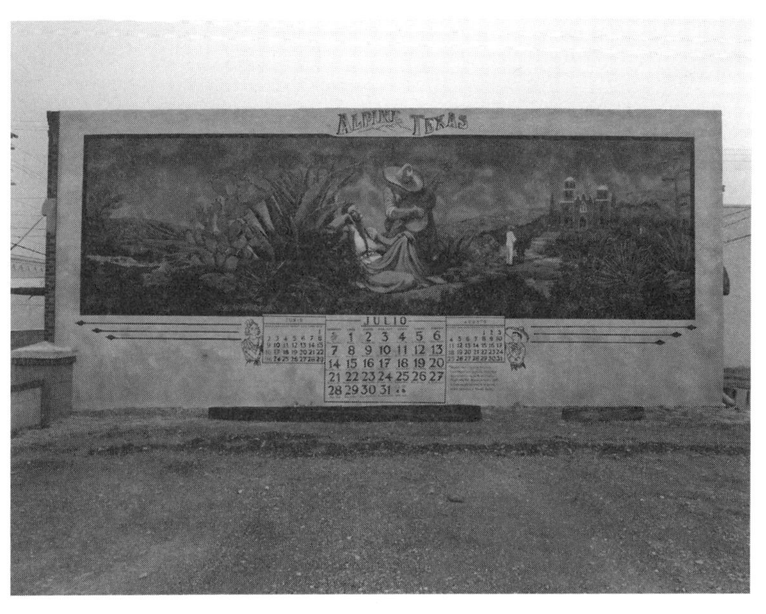
ALPINE TEXAS
JULIO
1 2 3 4 5 6
7 8 9 10 11 12 13
14 15 16 17 18 19 20
21 22 23 24 25 26 27
28 29 30 31

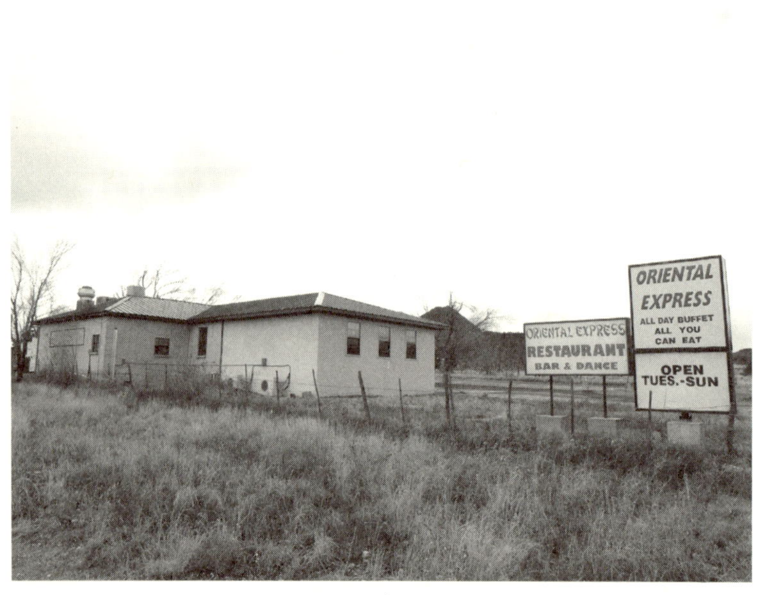
ORIENTAL EXPRESS
RESTAURANT
BAR & DANCE
ORIENTAL
EXPRESS
ALL DAY BUFFET
ALL YOU
CAN EAT
OPEN
TUES.-SUN

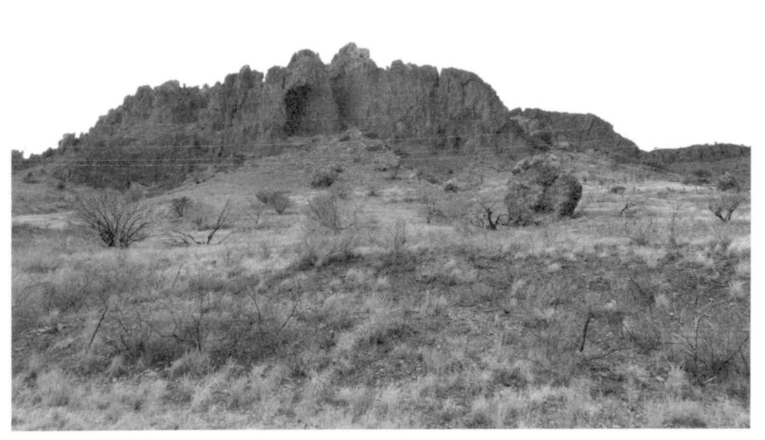

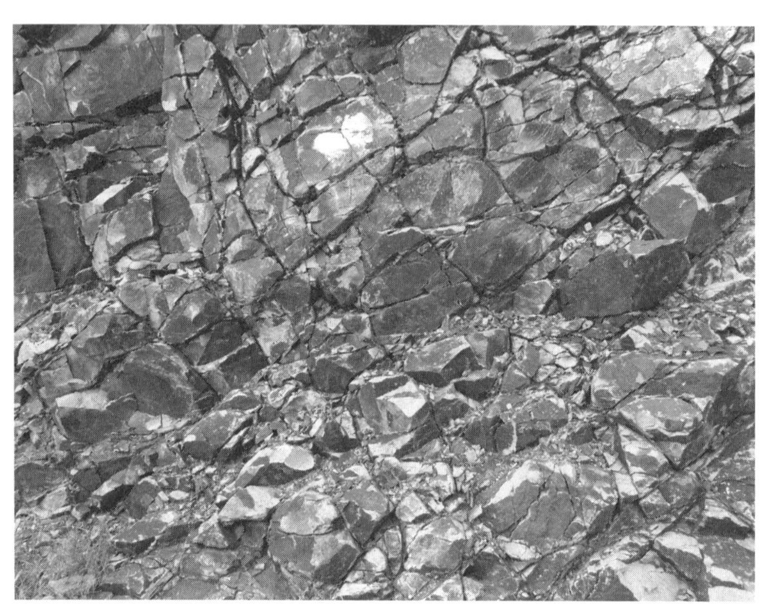

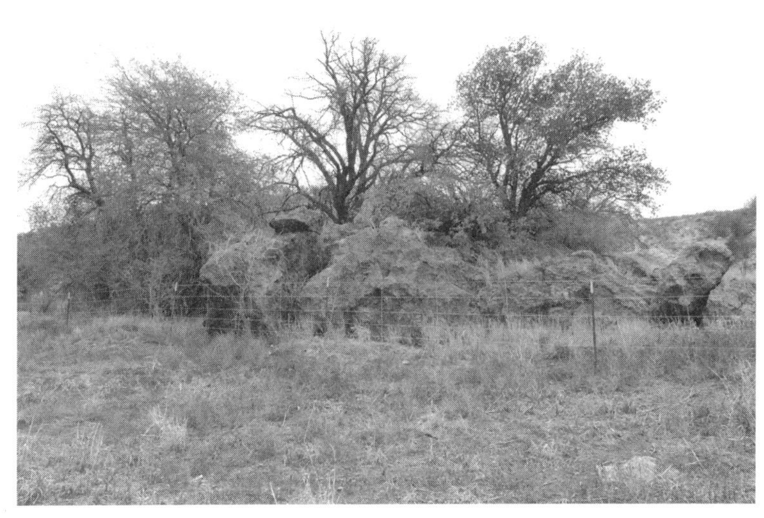

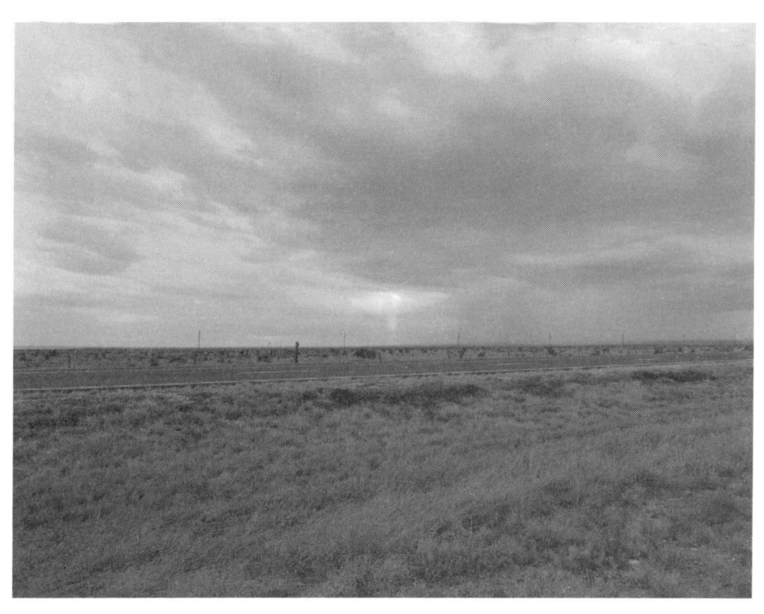

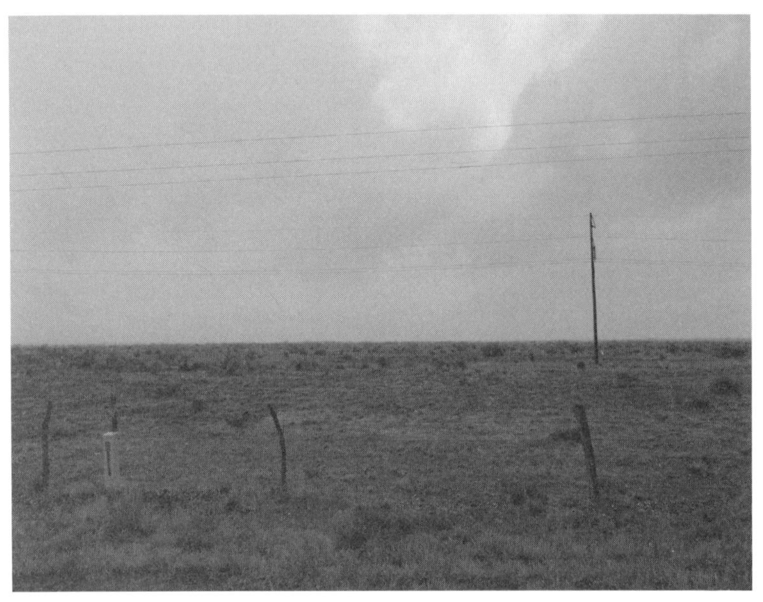

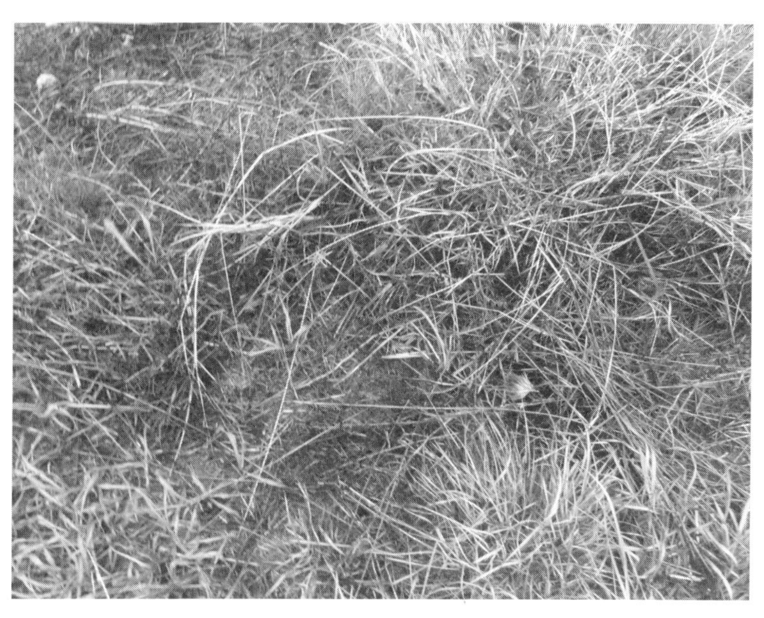

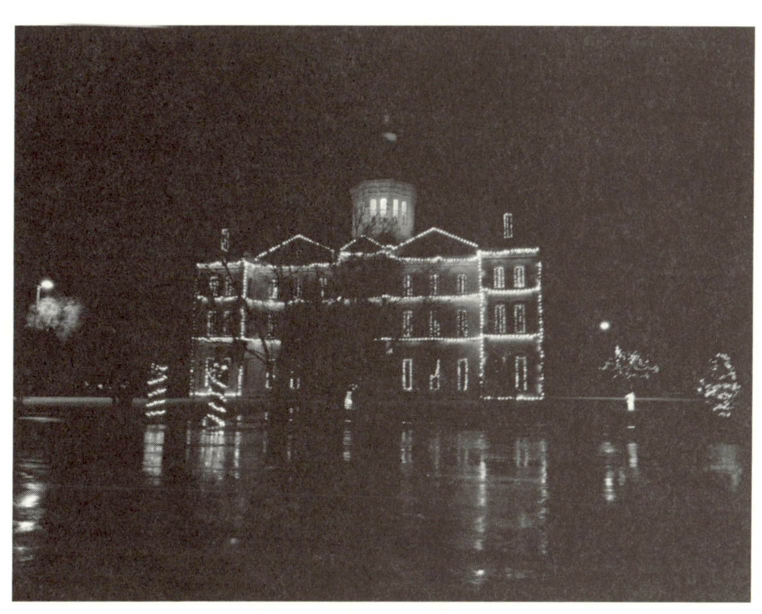

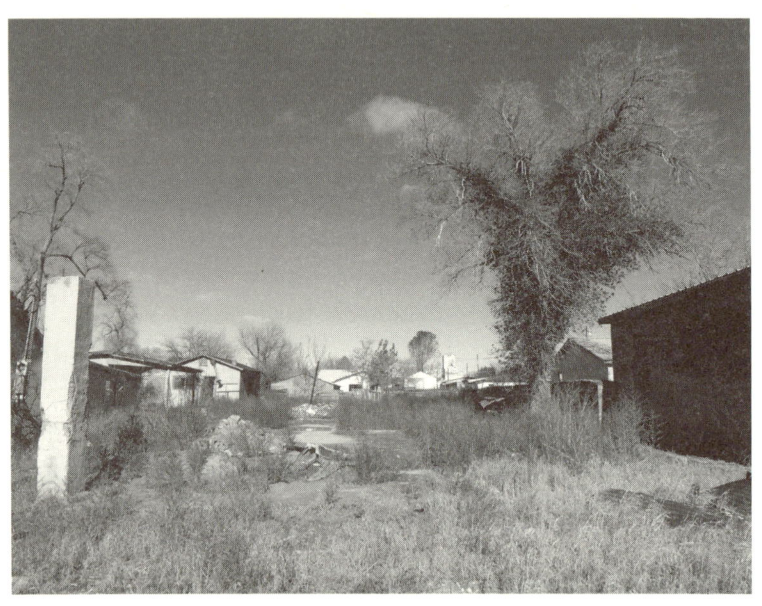

INDEX OF PHOTOGRAPHS

November 10 : 404 8th Street to Galveston Island State Park
1 (404 8th Street, Galveston), 2 (Avenue K), 3 (Seawall), 4 (Seascape),
5 (Three Pillars), 6 (Sunset)

November 11 : Galveston Island State Park to Surfside
7 (Sunrise), 8 (Seasacape), 9 (Seascape), 10 (Seascape),
11 (San Luis Pass), 12 (Seascape), 13 (Seascape), 14 (Seascape),
15 (Seascape), 16 (Seascape)

November 12 : Surfside to West Columbia
17 (Tree Line), 18 (Waterway), 19 (Waterway), 20 (Landscape),
21 (Tree Line), 22 (Sign and Horses), 23 (Landscape), 24 (Fence Line),
25 (Statue at Night), 26 (Gas Station at Night), 27 (Sign at Night)

November 13 : West Columbia to Needville
28 (Landscape), 29 (Tree), 30 (Landscape), 31 (Bobcat),
32 (Landscape), 33 (Landscape), 34 (School), 35 (Shed at Night)

November 14 : Needville to East Bernard
36 (Landscape), 37 (Building), 38 (Landscape), 39 (Landscape),
40 (Industrial Building), 41 (Landscape)

November 15 : East Bernard to Eagle Lake
42 (Farm Vehicles), 43 (Trees), 44 (Branches), 45 (Silos),
46 (Industrial Building), 47 (Landscape)

November 16 : Eagle Lake to Columbus
48 (Bird), 49 (Bird), 50 (Landscape with Cattle), 51 (Bird),
52 (Overpass), 53 (Crossroads)

November 17 : Columbus to La Grange
54 (Landscape), 55 (Trash), 56 (Pump Station), 57 (Landscape),
58 (Rectangle), 59 (Bones), 60 (Headless Deer), 61 (Hotel)

November 18 : La Grange to Buescher State Park
62 (Tree Line), 63 (Gate), 64 (Tractors), 65 (Tree Brace), 66 (Train), 67 (River)

November 19 : Buescher State Park to Bastrop
68 (Lake), 69 (Pond), 70 (Burnt Forest), 71 (Burnt Forest), 72 (Lake), 73 (River), 74 (Landscape), 75 (Campfire)

November 20 : Bastrop to Austin International Airport
76 (Sign), 77 (Road Stripe), 78 (Three Graves), 79 (Overpass), 80 (Hotel)

November 21 : Austin International Airport to Austin
81 (River), 82 (Capitol)

November 23 : Austin to Dripping Springs
83 (Vacant Building), 84 (Overpass), 85 (Rock), 86 (Grass), 87 (Reflection)

November 24 : Dripping Springs to Johnson City
88 (Brush), 89 (Fence), 90 (Bones), 91 (Tire), 92 (Creek), 93 (Sign), 94 (Creek), 95 (Landscape), 96 (Shrub at Night)

November 25 : Johnson City to Stonewall
97 (Mailboxes), 98 (Flag and Fence), 99 (Burnt Log), 100 (Landscape), 101 (Stone Wall)

November 26 : Stonewall to Fredericksburg
102 (Reflection), 103 (Tree and Building), 104 (Windmill), 105 (Historical Marker), 106 (Painting in Restaurant)

November 27 : Fredericksburg to Kerrville
107 (Shetland Pony), 108 (Landscape), 109 (Fenceline), 110 (Landscape), 111 (Landscape), 112 (Road), 113 (Landscape), 114 (825 Wheless Avenue, Kerrville)

December 4 : Kerrville to I-10 Frontage Road & US-290
115 (Lake), 116 (Industrial Building), 117 (Historical Marker), 118 (Feathers), 119 (Sky), 120 (Tree), 121 (Landscape), 122 (Landscape), 123 (Landscape)

December 5 : I-10 & US-290 to Junction
124 (Tree), 125 (Sky), 126 (Corral), 127 (Stone), 128 (Landscape with Steer), 129 (Landscape), 130 (Silo)

December 7 : Junction to Ranch Road 3130 & Private Road 3389
131 (Ice), 132 (Utility Box), 133 (Landscape), 134 (Landscape), 135 (Landscape), 136 (Bottle), 137 (Stone Wall), 138 (Road), 139 (Piece of Wood), 140 (Shrub)

December 8 : Ranch Road 3130 & Private Road 3389 to Sonora
141 (Leaves), 142 (Landscape with Steer), 143 (Sun), 144 (Fence), 145 (Landscape), 146 (Power Line), 147 (Reflector), 148 (Landscape), 149 (Sonora City Hall)

December 9 : Sonora to I-10 & Taylor Road
150 (Ice), 151 (Landscape), 152 (Cacti and Rocks), 153 (Landscape), 154 (Landscape), 155 (Landscape), 156 (Tree), 157 (Shrub), 158 (Landscape), 159 (Car Museum)

December 10 : I-10 & Taylor Road to Ozona
160 (Substation), 161 (Statue of Davy Crockett)

December 12 : Ozona to US-190 & Unmarked Ranch Road
162 (Natural Gas Silos), 163 (Sky), 164 (Cow), 165 (Landscape), 166 (Fence), 167 (Bungee Cord), 168 (Landscape), 169 (Culvert)

December 13 : US-190 & Unmarked Ranch Road to Iraan
170 (Cacti and Tree), 171 (Corral), 172 (Landscape), 173 (Road), 174 (Sky), 175 (Landscape), 176 (Roadside Memorial), 177 (Alley Oop Fantasy Land)

December 15 : Iraan to I-10 Frontage Road & Exit 285
178 (Restland Cemetary), 179 (Pumpjack), 180 (Landscape),
181 (Landscape), 182 (Thorns), 183 (Marker), 184 (Landscape),
185 (Wooden Wheel), 186 (Mountain), 187 (Cactus), 188 (Tree)

December 16 : I-10 Frontage Road & Exit 285 to Fort Stockton
189 (Rocks), 190 (Landscape), 191 (Landscape), 192 (Piece of Wood),
193 (Underpass), 194 (Century Plants), 195 (Landscape), 196 (Trash),
197 (Vacant Motel)

December 18 : Fort Stockton to Old Alpine Highway & US-67
198 (Feed Store), 199 (Landscape), 200 (Pecan Grove), 201 (Fence Post),
202 (Rock), 203 (Railroad Tracks), 204 (Century Plants), 205 (Rocks),
206 (Grass and Dirt), 207 (Sunset)

December 19 : Old Alpine Highway & US-67 to Alpine
208 (Dead Coyote), 209 (Landscape), 210 (Tumble Weed),
211 (Landscape), 212 (Landscape), 213 (Cardboard Box), 214 (Road),
215 (Gate), 216 (Landscape), 217 (Ground), 218 (Night Sky)

December 20 : Alpine to Marfa
219 (Mural), 220 (Restaurant), 221 (Landscape), 222 (Rock Wall),
223 (Landscape), 224 (Fabric), 225 (Landscape), 226 (Landscape),
227 (Grass), 228 (Distant Lights), 229 (Presidio County Courthouse)

December 21 : Marfa
230 (404 West Galveston Street, Marfa)

ACKNOWLEDGMENTS

These photographs and the walk during which they were taken were made possible with the generous support of the Akademie Schloss Solitude. My gratitude to Jean-Baptiste Joly, Silke Pflüger, Marieanne Roth, Angela Butterstein, Ingeburg Wohlgemuth, Konstantin Lom, Anita Carey-Yard, Horst Kaag, Ernst Ludwig, Sophie-Charlotte Thieroff, and the rest of the staff and fellows.

Thank you to everyone who supported the project by walking, providing lodging, and ordering photographs: John Alexander, Sam Amadon, Ayelet Amittay, Caleb Anderson, Anna Barker, Chloë Bass, Cathy Bennett, John Bennett, Noam Biale, Hal Boggess, Shelley Boggess, Camp Bosworth, Charlotte Boulay, Manuel Boutet, Suzanne Buffam, Ricard Bullock, Jason Canniff, Ross Cashiola, Daniel Cecil, Kishu Chand, Jenny Chio, Marcus Cooksey, Liz Countryman, Charlotte Cowden, Casey Cutler, Sara Cutler, Giulio Chiarenza, Megan Chiarenza, Jim Datz, Michael Tod Edgerton, Deborah Edwards, Van Edwards, Christoff Engbrecht, Yixin Fang, Robert Fernandez, Evan Firestone, Layla Forrest-White, David Brynjar Franzson, Gustavo Fricke, Saul Friedlander, Teresa Gallagher-Bell, Evan Gardner, Megan Garr, Dylan Gautier, Ross Greenspan, Jane Gregory, Louis Gropman, Mary Hickman, John Hogan, John Howell, Nancy Howell, Kate Ingold, Tim Johnson, Okey Johnson, Kathleen Johnson, Buck Johnston, Jean-Baptiste Joly, Brendan Jones, Carly Jones, Natali Jones, Addie Juell, Katie Kadue, Eugene Kang, Amir Kenan, Orna Kenan, Eric Kjensrud, Kraig Kraft, Jamie Krolikowski, Jean Landry, Jaslyn Law, Marshall Lee, Hai Liu, Rebecca Loewen, Joseph Mains, Micki McCoy, Mitch McEwan, James Meetze, Jeremy Melius, Andrew Moisey, Charlotte Moth, Nami Mun, Caitlin Murray, Sawako Nakayasu, Meghan O'Rourke, ozz, Maureen Paley, Joaquin Palomino, Gina Patnaik, Jeff Pecarovich, Ariel Perloff, Katie Peterson, Alex Pihut, Katie Pope, Mike Quaranto, Blaire Quaranto, Srikanth Reddy,

Naomi Reis, Leslie Renfro, John Romanek, Calle Rönnow, Gus Rose, Reverend Rupert, Robyn Schiff, Simona Schneider, Sam Schonzeit, Lisa Schumaier, Michelle Schwien, Jay Schwien, Brandon Shimoda, Geoffrey Shullenberger, Michael Stewart, Justin St. Germain, Kendra Sullivan, Lexi Suppes, Bronwen Tate, Claire Titleman, Stacey Tran, Nick Twemlow, Michelle Ty, David Vandeloo, Charlotte Whittle, Michael Williams, Alan Worn, Sandy Wu, Chengyi Xu, Seigo Yano, Zi Yin, Kyoko Yoshida, and Jia Zhang.

Most of all, thanks to Lynn Xu, my intrepid partner and guide for this walk and countless others.

Joshua Edwards directs and co-edits Canarium Books. He's the author of three collections of poetry, *Architecture for Travelers* (Edition Solitude, 2014), *Imperial Nostalgias* (Ugly Duckling Presse, 2013), and *Campeche* (Noemi Press, 2011), and the translator of Mexican poet María Baranda's *Ficticia* (Shearsman Books, 2010). Born on Galveston Island, he now lives in Marfa, Texas, with his wife, Lynn Xu.

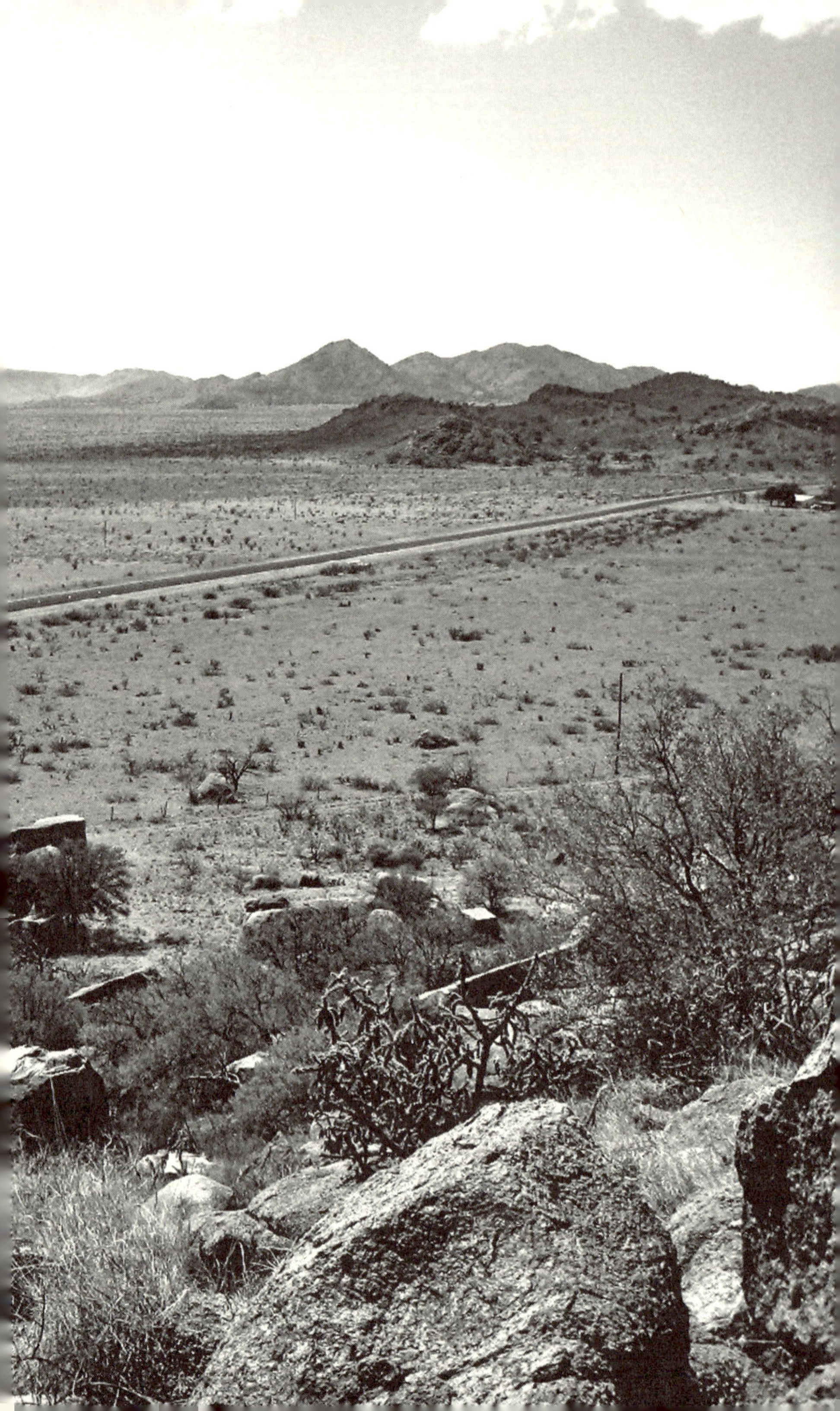